ANOTHER 50 TIPS & TRICKS FOR DYNAMICS AX 2012

BY MURRAY FIFE

ISBN: 1497383412

ISBN-13: 978-1497383418

Preface

What You Need For This Guide

All the examples shown in this blueprint were done with the Microsoft Dynamics AX 2012 virtual machine image that was downloaded from the Microsoft CustomerSource or PartnerSource site. If you don't have your own installation of Microsoft Dynamics AX 2012, you can also use the images found on the Microsoft Learning Download Center or deployed through Lifecycle Services. The following list of software from the virtual image was leveraged within this guide:

Microsoft Dynamics AX 2012 R3

Even though all the preceding software was used during the development and testing of the recipes in this book, they may also work on earlier versions of the software with minor tweaks and adjustments, and should also work on later versions without any changes.

Errata

Although we have taken every care to ensure the accuracy of our content, mistakes do happen. If you find a mistake in one of our books—maybe a mistake in the text or the code—we would be grateful if you would report this to us. By doing so, you can save other readers from frustration and help us improve subsequent versions of this book. If you find any errata, please report them by emailing editor@dynamicsaxcompanions.com.

Piracy

Piracy of copyright material on the Internet is an ongoing problem across all media. If you come across any illegal copies of our works, in any form, on the Internet, please provide us with the location address or website name immediately so that we can pursue a remedy.

Please contact us at legal@dynamicsaxcompanions.com with a link to the suspected pirated material.

We appreciate your help in protecting our authors, and our ability to bring you valuable content.

Questions

You can contact us at help@dynamicsaxcompanions.com if you are having a problem with any aspect of the book, and we will do our best to address it.

Table Of Contents

INTRODUCTION

Dynamics is a great product, because anyone is able to master the basics with just a little bit of a test drive. As you use it more, you will probably stumble on feature that no-one mentioned that makes Dynamics AX even better, and you store it away in your back pocket to use later on. The more you use the system, the more of these you will find, and with enough of these you turn from just a User to a Power User.

After releasing the initial set of tips and tricks, I realized that I had enough additional tips for a second volume containing 50 more tricks and tips that you can take advantage of within Dynamics AX. They range from tips on tweaking the Dynamics AX client to some of the hidden features within Dynamics AX itself that you may not know you can do. They also include tips on how to use other tools that are available to you to report better from the system, and how to use the office suite to really power charge Dynamics AX.

You will definitely find at least one or two more tips that will make your life easier.

DESKTOP CLIENT TIPS

You don't have to go very far within Dynamics AX to start finding features that can make your work a little easier because the desktop client itself is jam packed with features. You can tweak how the client looks so that you can see just the information that you want to see, and you can also use inbuilt shortcuts within the client to make finding information and getting around the system even easier.

Set Your Home Page To Automatically Refresh

The Home page within Dynamics AX is one of the most useful pages there is, because it gives you one place that you can go to in order to see everything that you are interested in. You can make it even more useful by having the page set to automatically refresh periodically so that you don't have to click the F5 button to refresh the page manually.

Now you will always up to date.

Set Your Home Page To Automatically Refresh

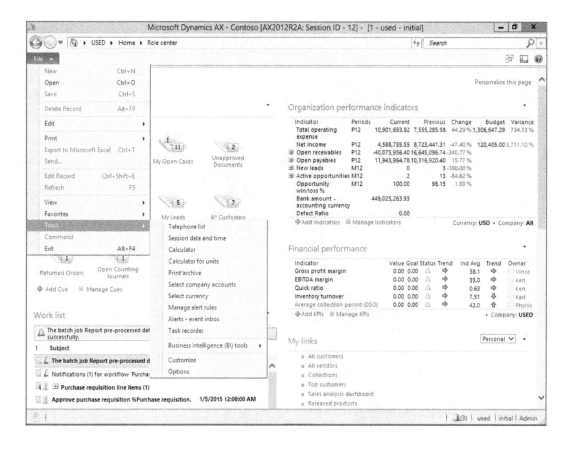

From the File menu, select the Tools submenu, and then click on the Options menu item.

Set Your Home Page To Automatically Refresh

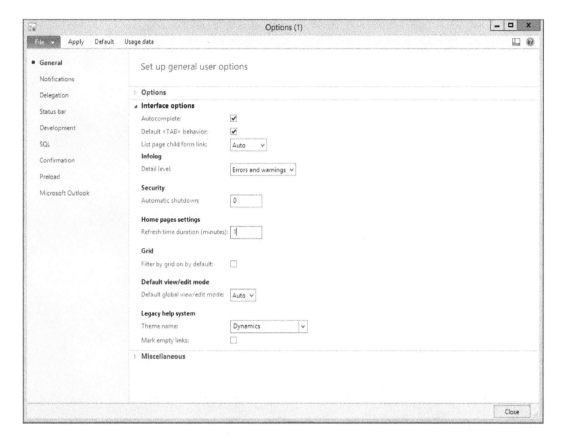

When the Options form is displayed, change the Refresh duration value within the Home page settings group of the General tab from 0 to the interval in minutes that you want have your home page refreshed, and then click on the Close button.

Set Your Home Page To Automatically Refresh

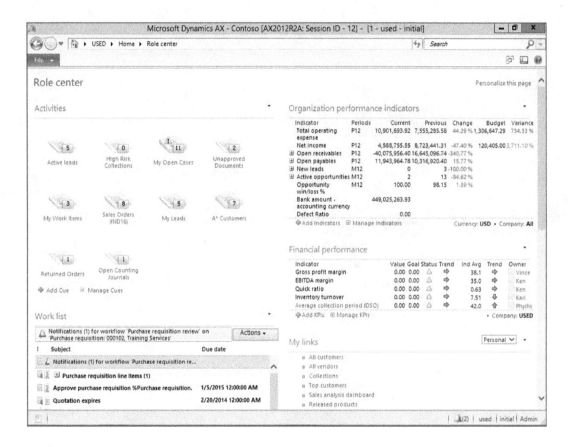

Now just wait and it will refresh automatically.

Change Your Company Through The Status Bar Charm

You all probably know how to change the company through the breadcrumb bar, but you can also change the company through the charm on the status bar. This option also gives you the ability to create a new workspace for the new company as well, just in case you need to have them both open at once.

You can now change companies faster than Worzel Gummidge changed his head.

Change Your Company Through The Status Bar Charm

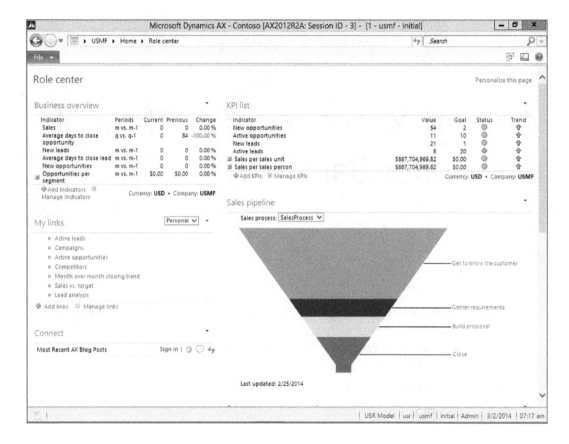

If you look at the status bar of the Dynamics AX client, then you will notice that the current Company is displayed there. Just double click on it.

Change Your Company Through The Status Bar Charm

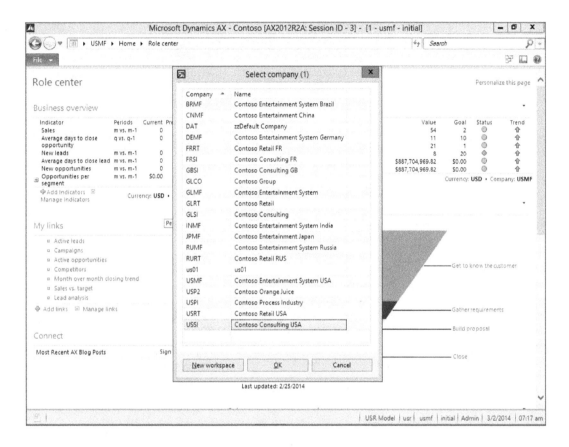

When the Select Company dialog box is displayed, you will see all of the companies that you have access to and you can just select the new company and click the OK button to switch within your current workspace.

Alternatively, if you want to open up a new workspace for the company that you have selected, and keep your current company workspace open as well, then just click on the New Workspace button.

Change Your Company Through The Status Bar Charm

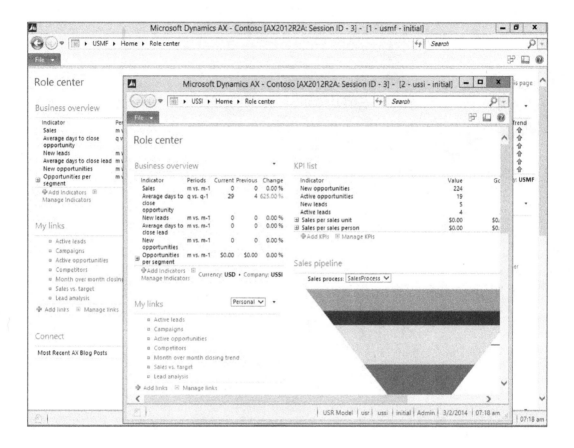

How easy is that.

Open New Workspaces To Quickly Access Multiple Areas At Once

Sometimes one version of Dynamics AX running on your desktop is just not enough. Rather than reaching for the desktop shortcut to start up another instance of the application, just create a new Workspace. They start up so much faster.

Open New Workspaces To Quickly Access Multiple Areas At Once

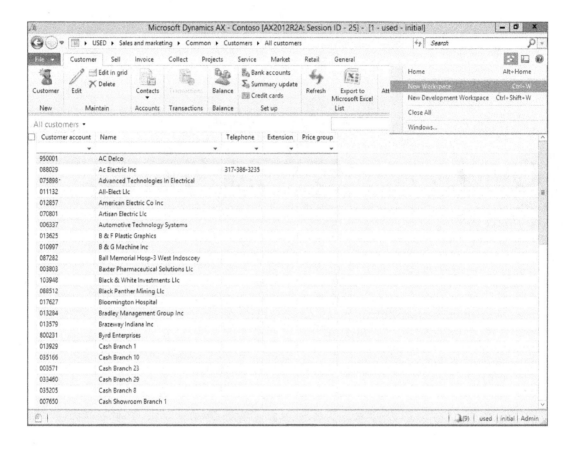

Click on the Windows icon in the top right of the Dynamics AX client, and select the New Workspace menu item (or press CTRL+W).

Open New Workspaces To Quickly Access Multiple Areas At Once

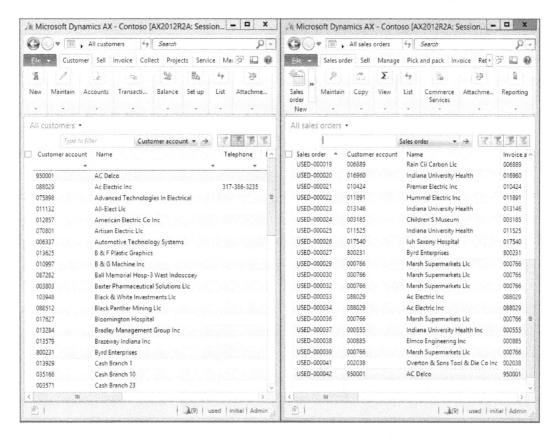

This will open up a new independent workspace that you can work with in addition to the original workspace.

Clean Up The Navigation Pad To Show Just The Modules You Need

The good thing about Dynamics AX is that you get all the available modules automatically. The downside is that you get all the available modules automatically. You may not want to see the General Ledger, or Accounts Payable modules, all you may be interested in may just be the Distribution modules.

You can quickly make your life a little less cluttered just by editing your Navigation Pad and hiding all of the modules that you don't need. You can still get to the functionality, just you don't need to wade through the other modules when trying to get to the menu items that you use every day.

Clean Up The Navigation Pad To Show Just The Modules You Need

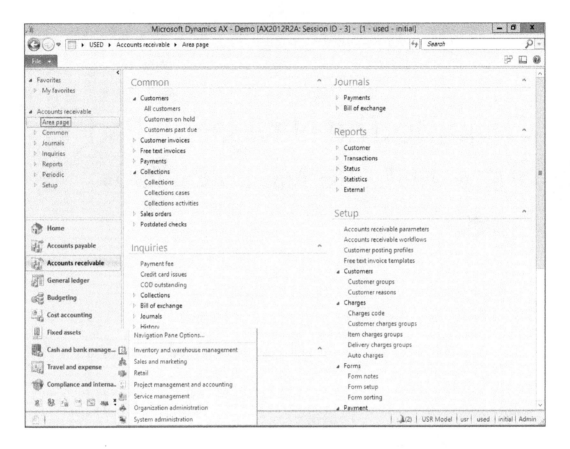

Click on the >> button at the bottom right of the Navigation Pad to see all of the additional modules, and then click on the Navigation Pane Options menu item.

Clean Up The Navigation Pad To Show Just The Modules You Need

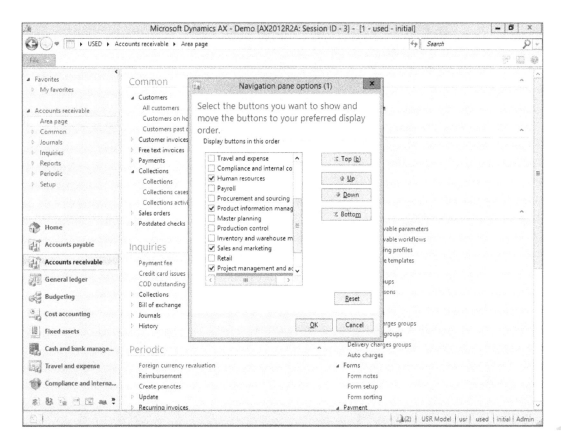

When the Navigation Pane Options window is displayed, you will see all of the modules that you have access to, and to remove them from the navigation pane, you just need to uncheck them.

When you have finished doing that, click on the OK button.

Clean Up The Navigation Pad To Show Just The Modules You Need

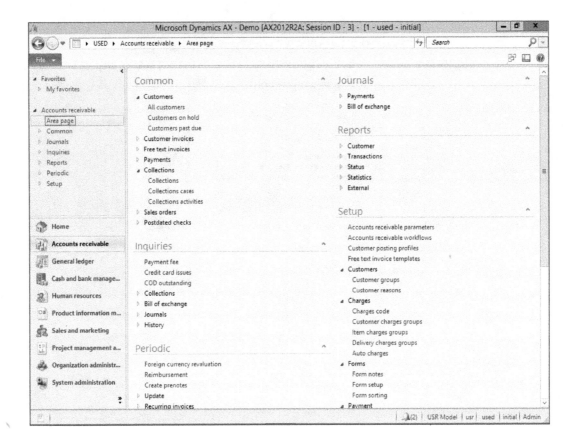

Now your Navigation Pane will look a lot tidier and you will have quick access to just the menu items that you are interested in.

Clean Up The Navigation Pad To Show Just The Modules You Need

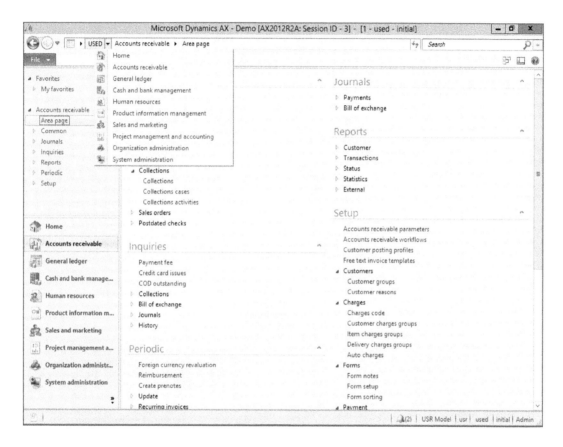

Also, this applies to the dropdown from the breadcrumb bar.

Add Entire Menu Item Groups At Once To Your Favorites Menu

Everyone is probably very familiar with the Favorites menu, and knows that you can add any menu item that you like there with just a click of the mouse. Did you know that you can also add groups of menu items as well, that copies all of the structure from the area page menu group over to your favorites as well.

By doing this you can avoid having to spend all that time creating your own personal menu groups in the favorites because they have already been grouped within the area page for you.

Add Entire Menu Item Groups At Once To Your Favorites Menu

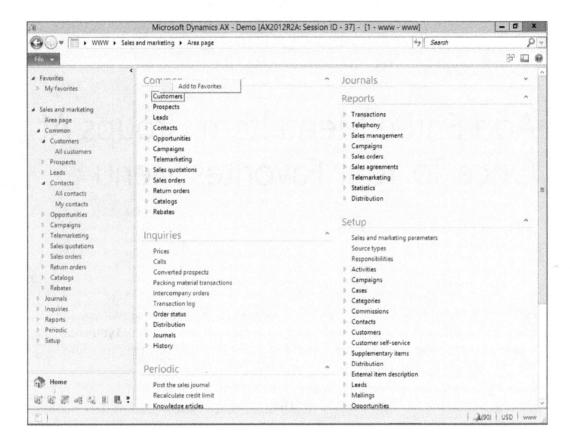

Right-mouse-click on the menu heading that you want to add to your favorites and select the Add to Favorites option. In this case I selected the Common group of the Sales and Marketing.

Add Entire Menu Item Groups At Once To Your Favorites Menu

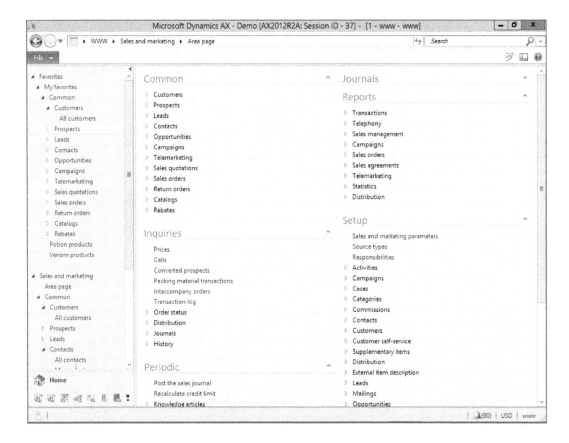

Now when you open up your favorites, the entire sub-menu will be there, including all of the child menu items.

Add Entire Menu Item Groups At Once To Your Favorites Menu

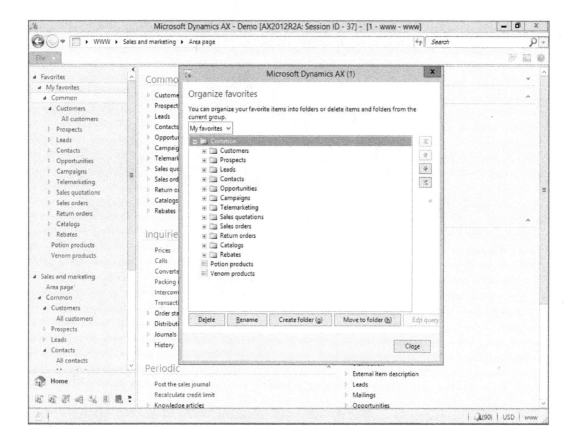

If you want to get rid of some of the submenus, then you can right-mouse-click on the My Favorites menu group, and select the Organize favorites option, which will show you the Organize favorites maintenance form.

Add Entire Menu Item Groups At Once To Your Favorites Menu

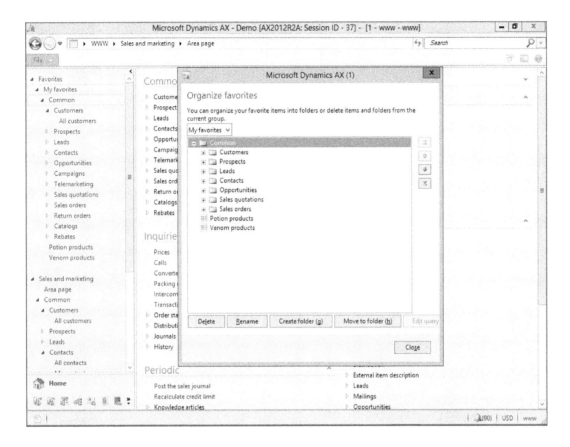

Once you have tweaked the menu structure to show just the information that you want then click on the Close button to save your changes.

Add Entire Menu Item Groups At Once To Your Favorites Menu

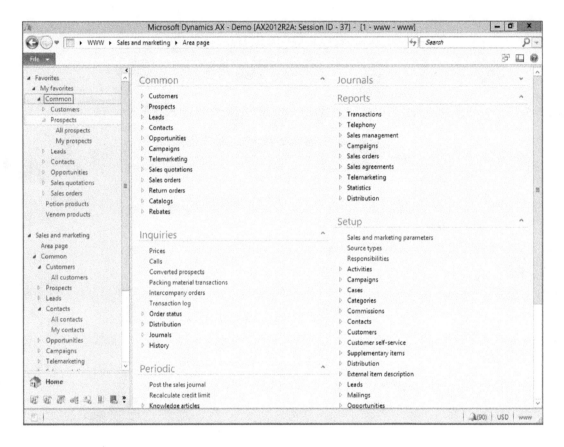

Now you will have all the menu items that you need from the area page group without having to add them all individually.

Hide The Navigation And Fact Box Panels For More Workspace

Although it's good to see the Navigation Bar and the Fact Box panes within Dynamics AX, sometimes you just need a little space so that you can see all the information that you are working on. That's OK though because you can turn those pane on and off through the View options within the Dynamics AX client.

Now all of you that are shouting "Show me the data!" can get back to work.

Hide The Navigation And Fact Box Panels For More Workspace

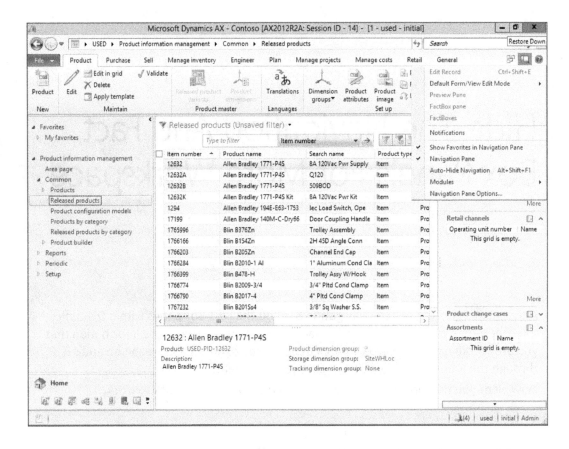

Open up the View options, either by clicking on it in the top right-hand corner of the Dynamics AX client, or by pressing ALT-V. From there you can toggle off the Fact pane and the Navigation pane just by selecting them.

Hide The Navigation And Fact Box Panels For More Workspace

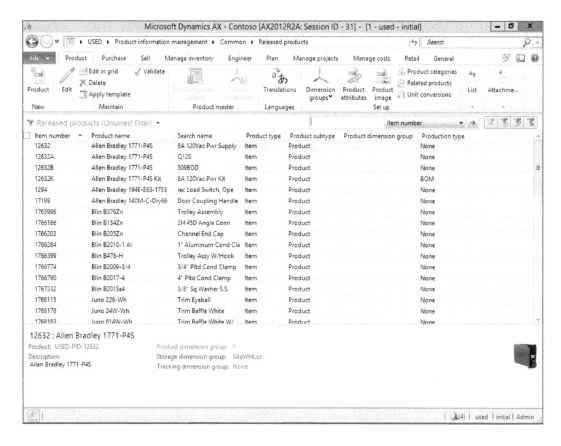

Now you have more space on your desktop.

Filter Your Favorites Menu Item

You all probably know that you can add any menu item link to your own personal favorites menu, but you don't have to stop there. You can personalize those favorites also to automatically apply a filter so that you get just the records back that you need.

By doing this, you can create multiple favorite links to the same menu item that returns different sets of data depending on what you are working on, saving you a few extra steps.

Filter Your Favorites Menu Item

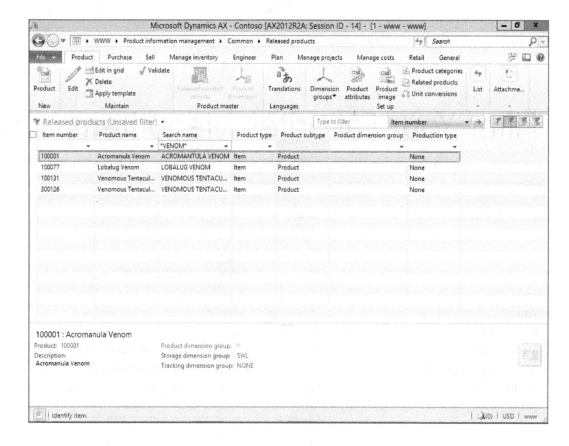

Start off by opening up the form that you want to create the favorites shortcut for, and filter the form to just the records that you want to have selected.

Filter Your Favorites Menu Item

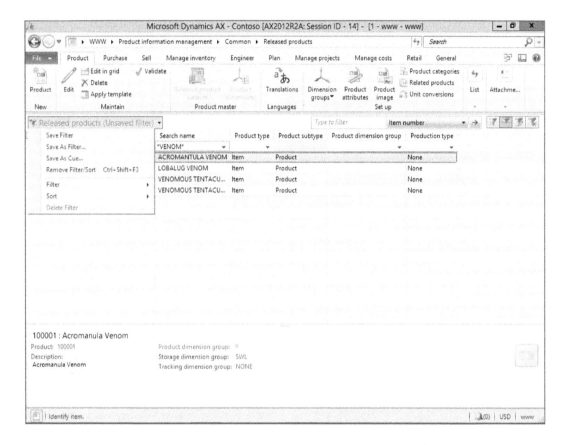

From the Filter menu, select the Save as Filter menu item.

Filter Your Favorites Menu Item

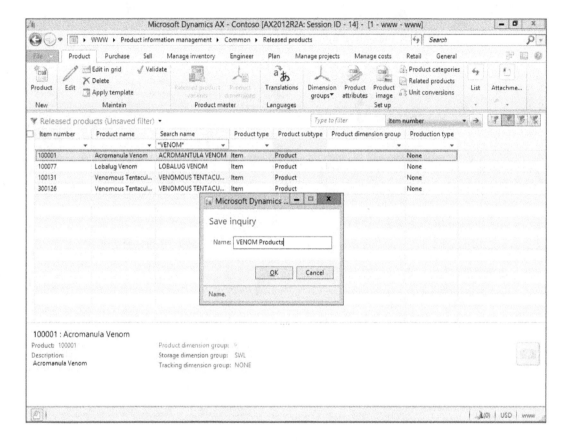

Then give your filter a Name and click the OK button to save the filter.

Filter Your Favorites Menu Item

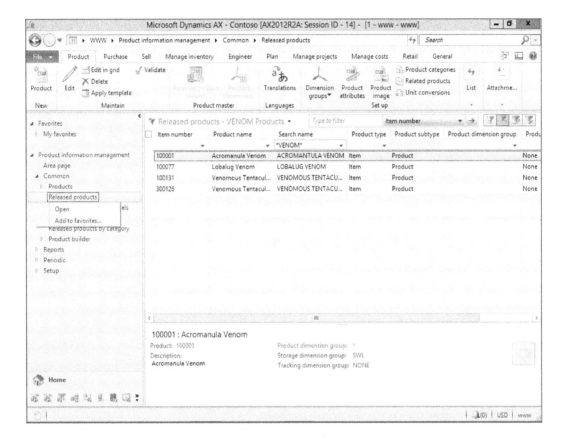

Now right-mouse-click on the parent form, and select the Add to favorites menu item.

Filter Your Favorites Menu Item

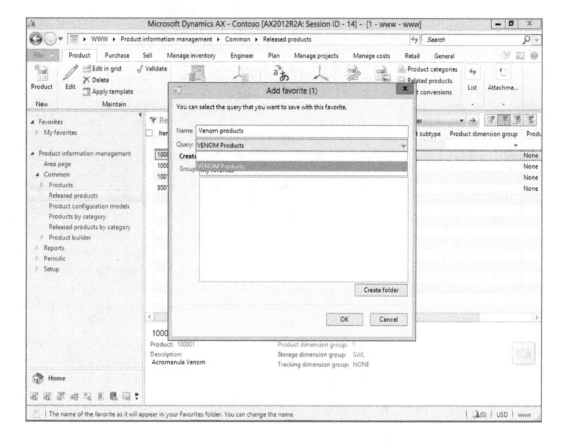

When the Add favorite dialog box is displayed, give your new favorite link a name, and then select the Query that you just created from the dropdown box.

Filter Your Favorites Menu Item

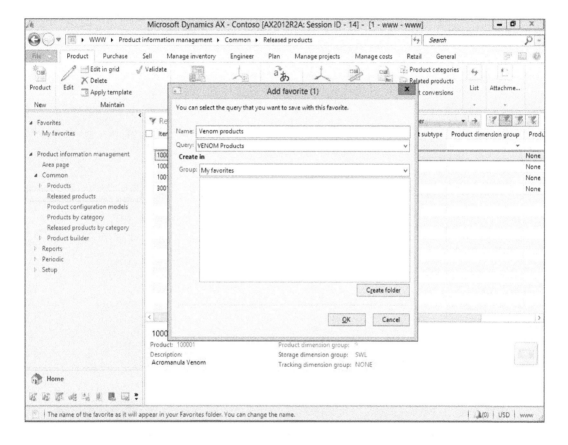

When you have done that, click on the OK button to save the filtered favorite.

Filter Your Favorites Menu Item

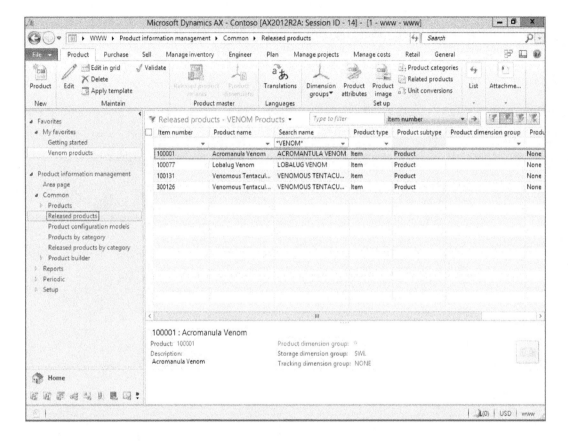

You can create multiple links to the same form, each with their own filters, so that you can quickly go to just the records that you want.

Navigate The Ribbon Bar Like A Street Fighter With Shortcut Keys

There are two types of users in the world. Those that are attached to their mouse and want to click through the application, and those that are attached to the keyboard and want to use shortcut keys to do everything. For the latter group, don't worry, you can navigate through Dynamics AX just as quickly with the keyboard.

With combo keys at your disposal you will be kicking butt like Ken & Ryu.

Navigate The Ribbon Bar Like A Street Fighter With Shortcut Keys

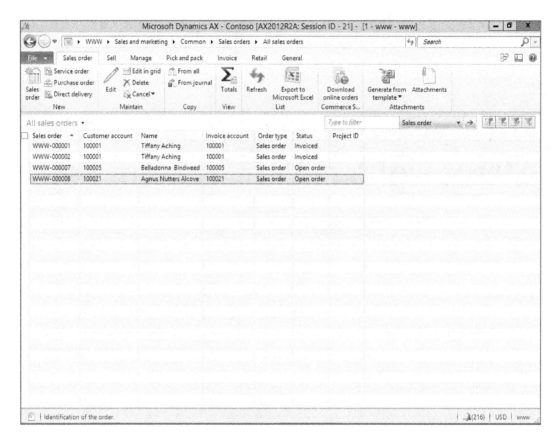

Start off by opening up the form that you want to navigate though. In this case we will use the shortcut keys to create a new Sales Order.

Navigate The Ribbon Bar Like A Street Fighter With Shortcut Keys

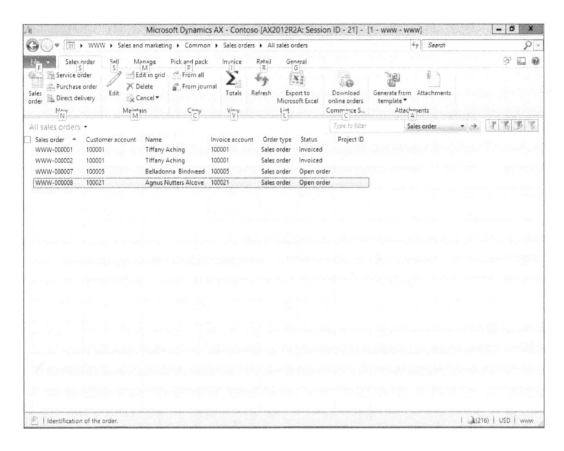

Press the ALT key and all of the shortcut options will be displayed on the screen. The first set will be for all of the ribbon bars and also all of the main groups within the selected ribbon bar.

Press N to select the New group of the Sales Order ribbon bar.

Navigate The Ribbon Bar Like A Street Fighter With Shortcut Keys

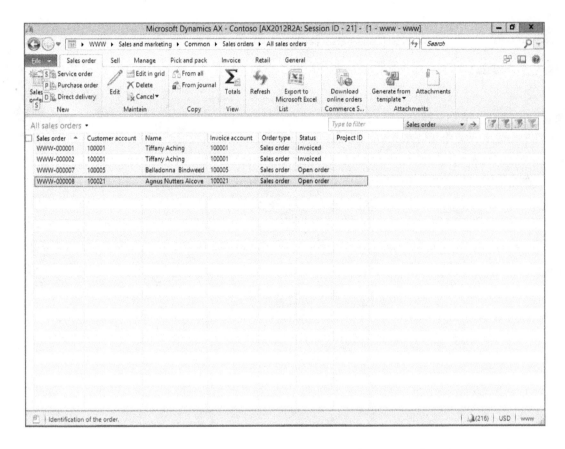

The shortcut options will change to just show the items that are within the group that you selected.

Press S.

Navigate The Ribbon Bar Like A Street Fighter With Shortcut Keys

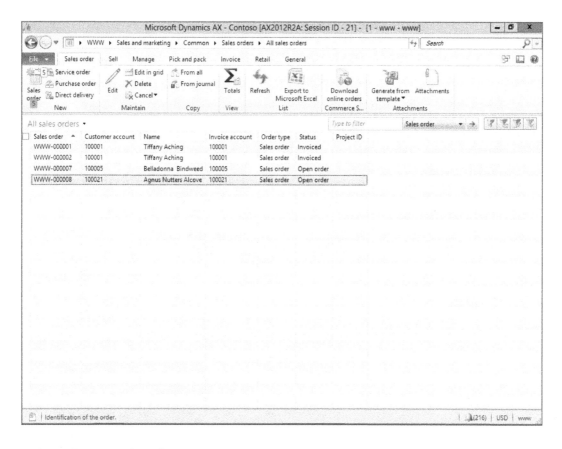

This will restrict the selections now to just the ones beginning with S. Note here that there are multiple options available. If you didn't want the Sales Order, then you can press S again to toggle to the next S option.

When you are on the right menu icon, just press Enter.

Navigate The Ribbon Bar Like A Street Fighter With Shortcut Keys

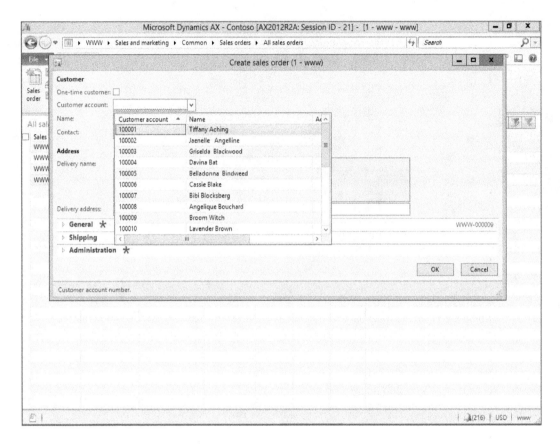

Now you will be in the Create Sales Order dialog box. Now all you have to remember for the next time that you want to create a new Sales Order is:

ALT, N, S, ENTER

How Easy is that!

Hack Form Selection Criteria For Mass Updates

Every now and then you may come across an update that has been designed to be performed one record at a time, and you have 10's, 100's, or even 1000's of records that you want to update at once. Even though it seems like all hope is lost and that you are going to end up with carpel tunnel syndrome from too many mouse clicks, it's not a bleak as you think.

There is a way that you can usually hack the selection query that is used by default for the form to widen up the range of records that will be updated at once. And it's pretty easy to do as well.

Hack Form Selection Criteria For Mass Updates

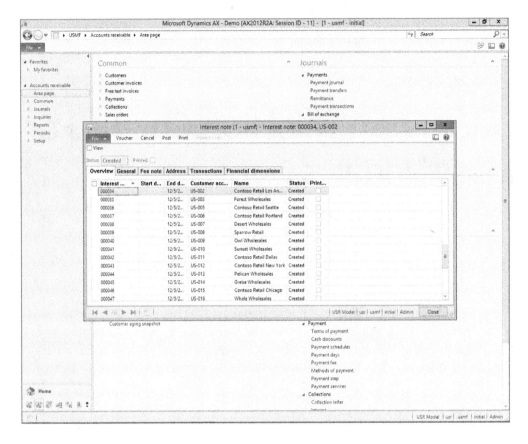

On some forms, if you select one record then you are able to use the menu items.

Hack Form Selection Criteria For Mass Updates

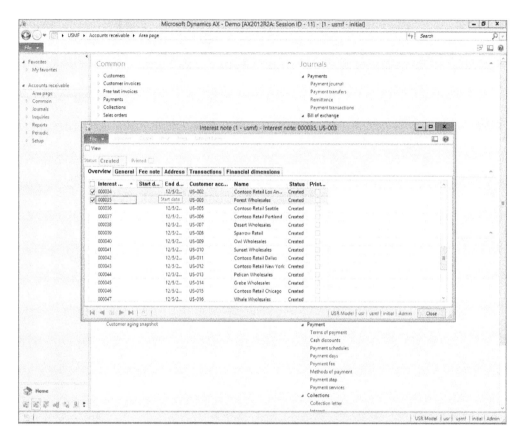

But if you select multiple records, then the menu's are disabled.

Hack Form Selection Criteria For Mass Updates

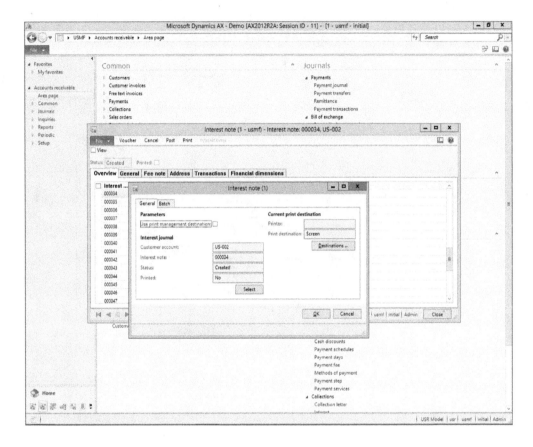

Select one record and click on the menu item that you want to apply to all of the records = in this case the Print option for the Interest Notes. Notice the selection criteria in the dialog form shows the record that will be used for this update.

Click on the Select button to change the selection criteria.

Hack Form Selection Criteria For Mass Updates

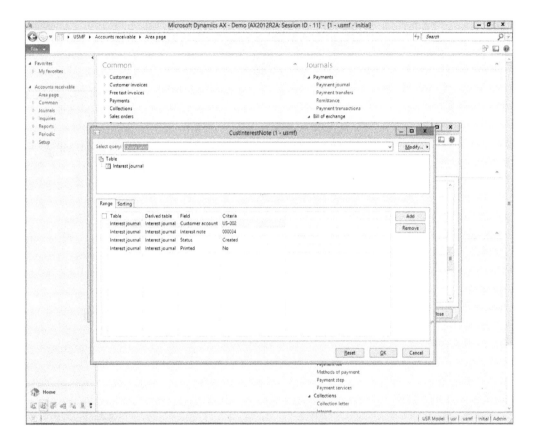

When the selection query editor is displayed you will be able to see the selection criteria records again.

Hack Form Selection Criteria For Mass Updates

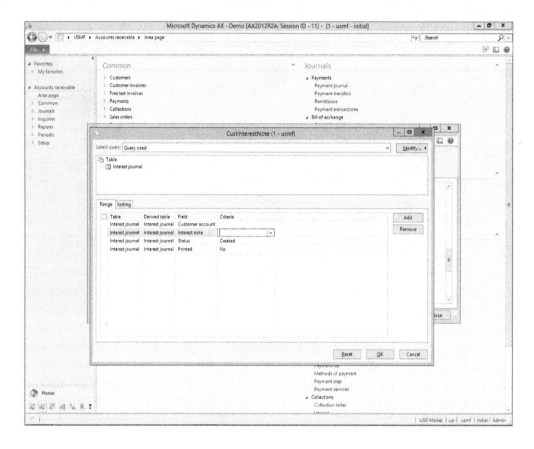

Blank out the fields that you don't want to filter on to open up the selection to a wider range of records and then click on the OK button.

Hack Form Selection Criteria For Mass Updates

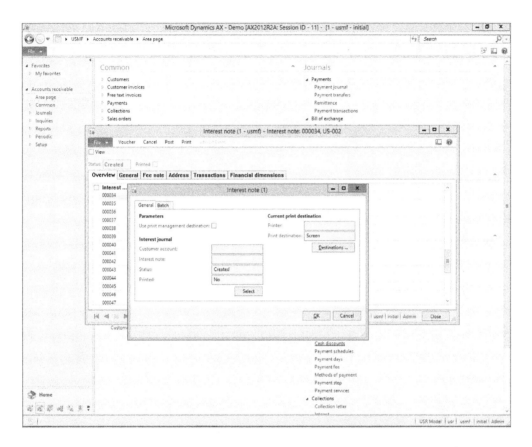

When you return to the selection dialog box you will notice that those field selections are now blank. Just click on the OK button to continue.

Hack Form Selection Criteria For Mass Updates

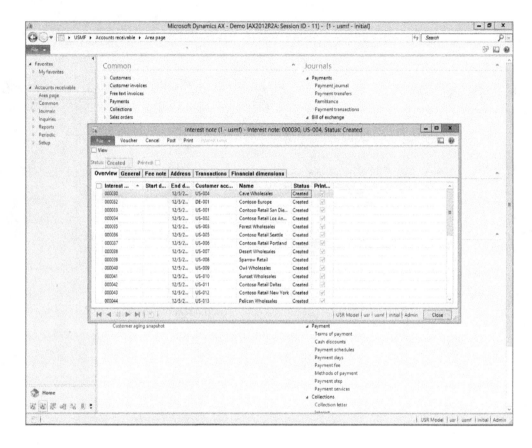

This will now perform the action that was only being allowed to be applied to the single record to all of the records that match the search range.

Copy Document Attachments From One Record To One Or More Other Records

Document attachments are a great feature within Dynamics AX, because it allows you to attach notes and files to almost any piece of data within the system. But don't reattach the same document over and over again if it applies to multiple records, use the copy and paste option that is built into the Document Management feature.

It's not plagiarizing to copy documents, it's just more efficient.

Copy Document Attachments From One Record To One Or More Other Records

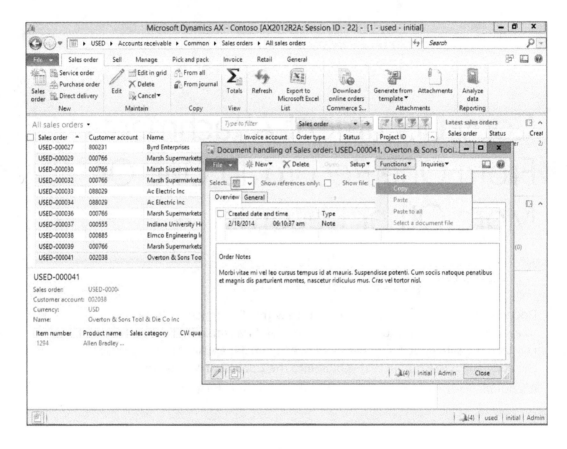

To copy an attachment from one record to another, open up the Document Handling form, select the attachments, and then select the Copy option from the Functions menu.

Copy Document Attachments From One Record To One Or More Other Records

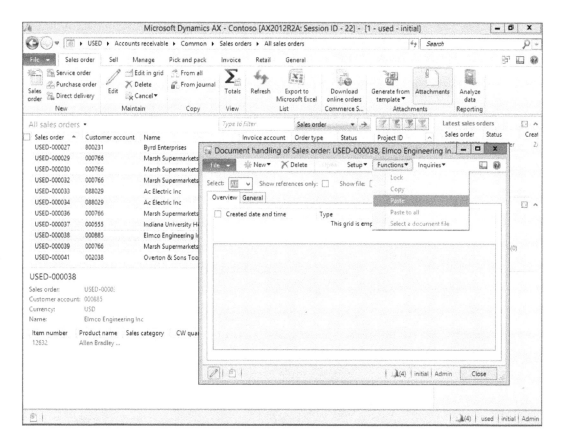

Then open up the Document Attachments form for the record that you want to attach the document to, and select the Paste option from the Functions menu.

Copy Document Attachments From One Record To One Or More Other Records

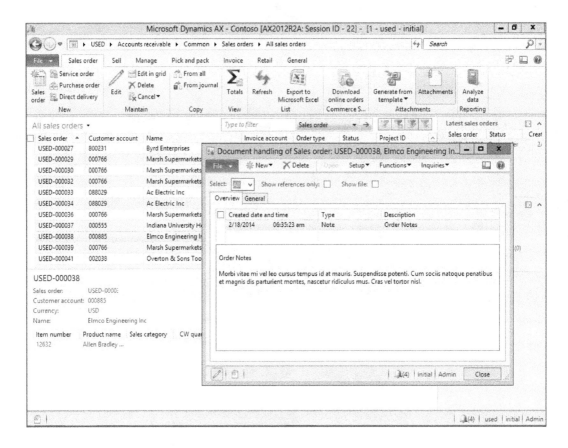

Now the document should be associated with the target record.

Copy Document Attachments From One Record To One Or More Other Records

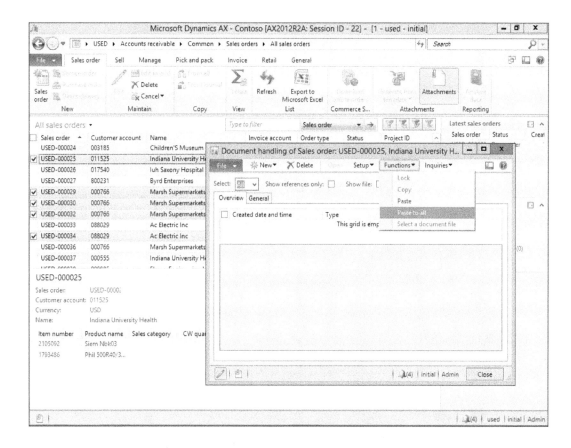

If you want to paste the attachment against multiple records at once, just select all of the records, open up the Document Attachments form, and then select the Paste To All option from within the Functions menu.

Copy Document Attachments From One Record To One Or More Other Records

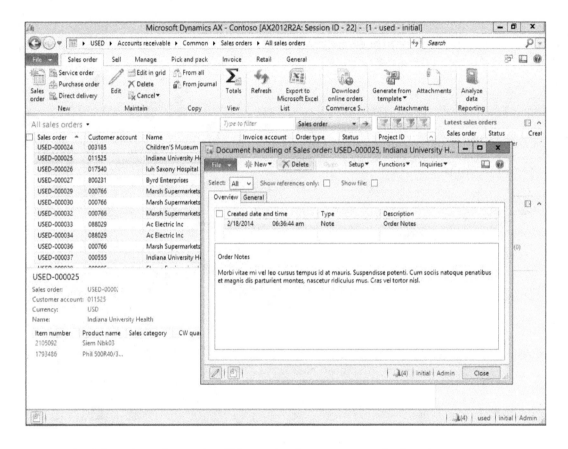

Now all of the selected records will have the document attached to them.

How easy is that.

Process Multiple Records At Once By Using The Multi-Select Option

A lot of the time you are not just working on one record at a time, you are processing batches of records. For example, you may be releasing multiple orders to picking, confirming multiple purchase orders, or printing multiple order confirmations. Dynamics AX makes this easy as pie to do because a lot of the time, you can use the multiple selection option to choose the records that you want to perform the same action on, and then it will work through them one at a time so that you don't have to.

Say goodbye to being stuck in the Groundhog Day equivalent of single record processing.

Process Multiple Records At Once By Using The Multi-Select Option

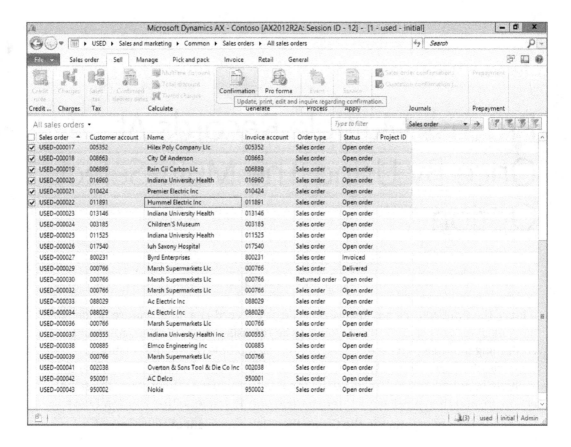

In this example we will show how you can generate multiple order confirmations with just the click of the button.

Just select all of the orders that you want to print, and then click on the Confirmation button within the Generate group of the Sell ribbon bar.

Process Multiple Records At Once By Using The Multi-Select Option

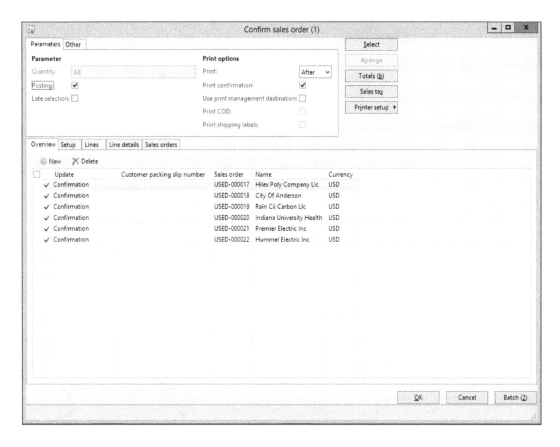

When the Confirm Sales Order dialog box is displayed, all of the orders will be shown in the detail section. All you need to do is click the OK button.

Process Multiple Records At Once By Using The Multi-Select Option

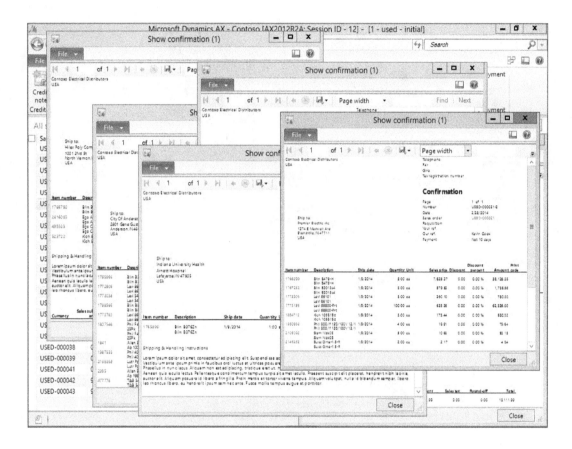

Now all of the order confirmations will be created.

If you used the email, or automatic printing option then this process would look a lot less cluttered ☺

Quickly Filter Your Data Through The Type To Filter Box

If you want to quickly filter list pages to show you just the records that you are interested in then Dynamics AX provides a Type to Filter option on almost all of the main forms. All you need to do is type in what you are looking for, and it will do the rest for you.

Getting rid of all the data that you don't want has never been so easy.

Quickly Filter Your Data Through The Type To Filter Box

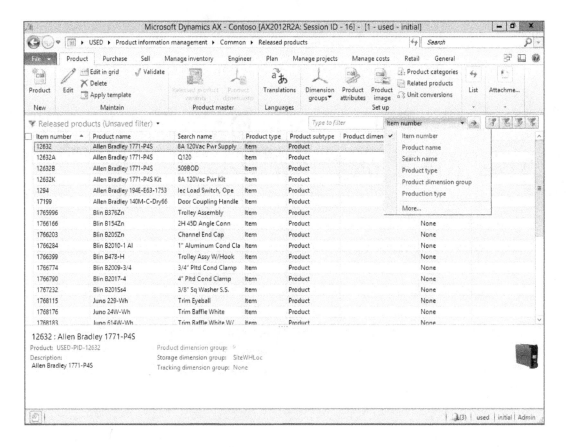

To filter your data, start off by clicking on the combo box to the right of the Type to Filter field, and selecting the field that you would like to filter on. All of the fields that are shown on the list page will be listed here.

Quickly Filter Your Data Through The Type To Filter Box

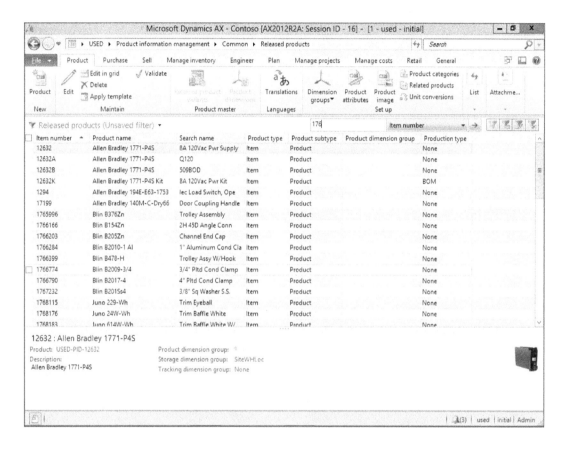

Then just select the Type to Filter field either by clicking on it with the mouse, or by using the SHIFT+F3 shortcut key, and then type in the key words that you want to filter your current list page on.

Quickly Filter Your Data Through The Type To Filter Box

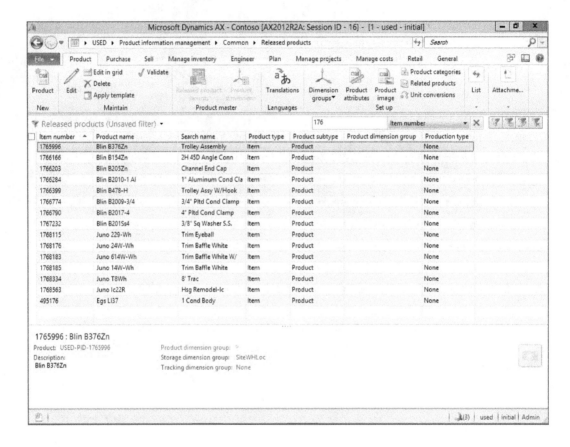

As soon as you press the Enter key, your view will be filtered, and return all records where the field contains your filter term.

Note: You won't have to type in any wild cards or use any placeholders in the search.

How simple is that?

Add New Fields To The Type To Filter Search Form To Find Hard To Find Data

The Type To Filter search option is super useful, but you are not limited to just the default fields that show up on the list page. If you want to search based on additional fields, then all you need to do is add them to the search criteria and then start searching.

No data is able to hide from you now.

Add New Fields To The Type To Filter Search Form To Find Hard To Find Data

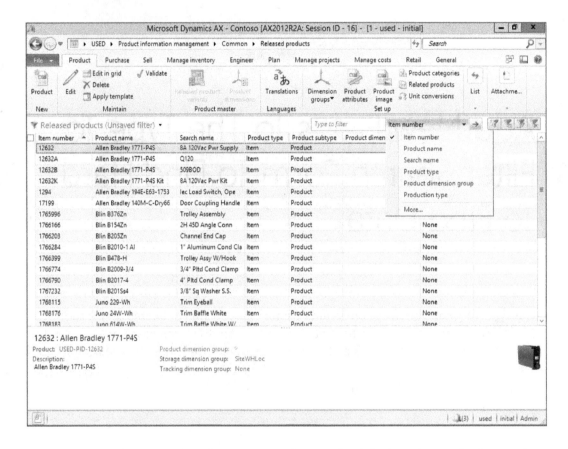

If you want to filter on a field that does not show up by default in the combo box to the right of the Type to Filter field, just click on the More option at the bottom of the list.

Add New Fields To The Type To Filter Search Form To Find Hard To Find Data

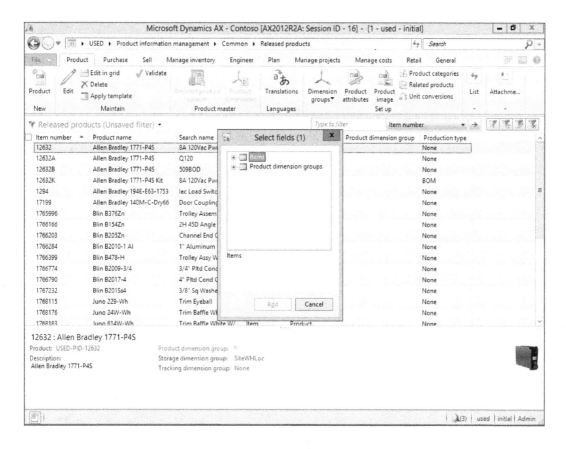

This will open up the Select Fields dialog box that will show you all of the tables that are related to the list page that you are currently in.

Add New Fields To The Type To Filter Search Form To Find Hard To Find Data

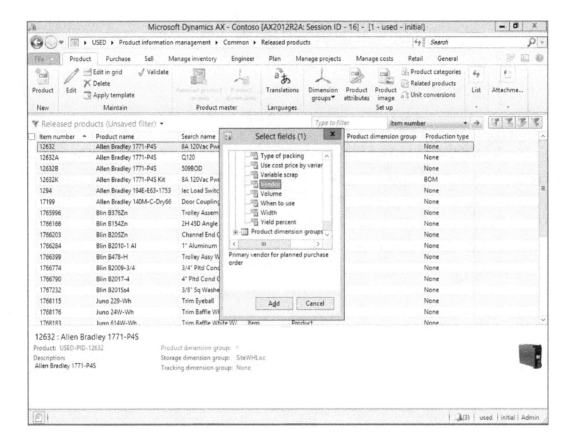

If you expand out the tables in the Select Fields dialog box, then you can select any additional field and then click the Add button.

After you have added all of the additional search fields, then just close the form.

Add New Fields To The Type To Filter Search Form To Find Hard To Find Data

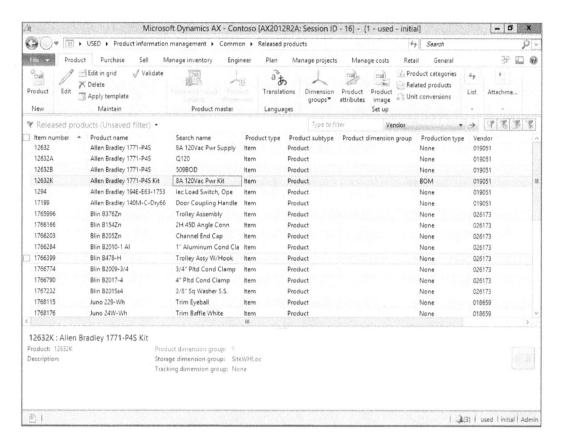

When you return to the list page, you will see all of the additional search fields have been added to the list page, and can also now be selected from the field drop down selector.

Add New Fields To The Type To Filter Search Form To Find Hard To Find Data

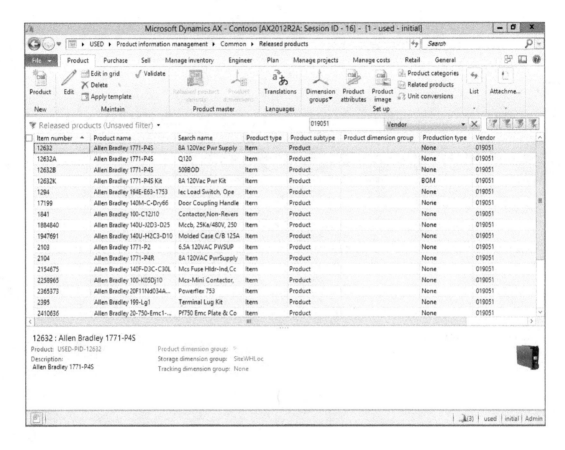

All you have to do in order to filter out based on the new fields is type in your search value, and the list page will be filtered.

Isn't that too cool?

Use Filter By Selection To Quickly Find Common Records

Filtering your list pages is even easier if you have an example of a record already on the page that matches what you are searching for because you can use it as a template for your search and use the Filter By Selection feature to find all of the other records that match, saving you a few extra keystrokes.

This feature will turn you into a data filtering Ninja.

Use Filter By Selection To Quickly Find Common Records

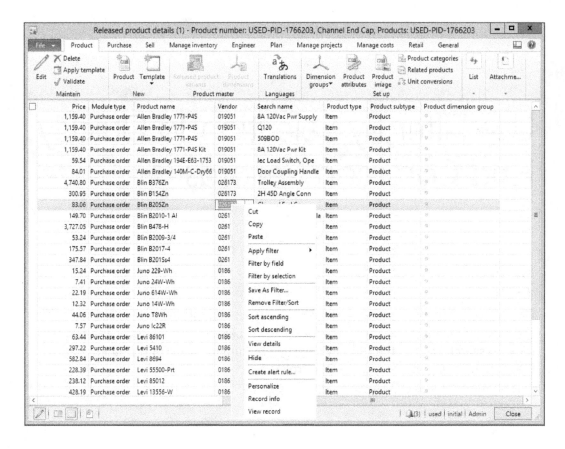

Just right-mouse-click on the field value that you want to filter based on, and then select the Filter By Selection option from the context menu.

Use Filter By Selection To Quickly Find Common Records

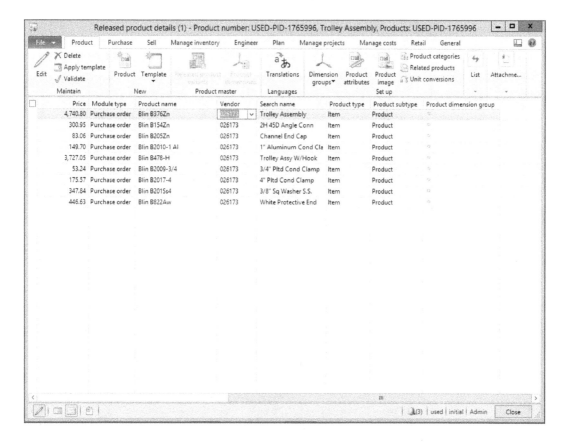

The list page will then be filtered to just the records that match that field value.

How easy was that!

Use The Filter by Field To Search For Subsets Of Data Within Columns

Sometimes, you just want to search for all records within a list page that match some sort of criteria. If this is the whole value of a field then you can use the Filter By Selection feature, but if you want to be a little more flexible, and maybe search for subsets of data within the field, then there is a better way to do it by using the Filter By Field feature.

Now you can extract out the data like a surgeon rather than a butcher.

Use The Filter by Field To Search For Subsets Of Data Within Columns

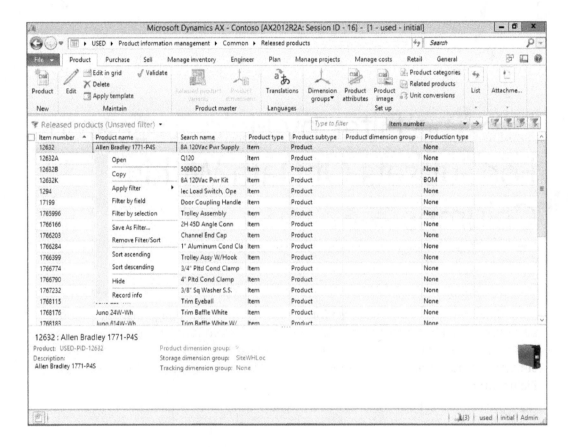

To quickly filter a column of data in a list page, just right-mouse-click on the field that you want to filter on, and then select the Filter by Field option from the sub-menu.

Alternatively, if your cursor is already on that field, then just press CTRL+F.

Use The Filter by Field To Search For Subsets Of Data Within Columns

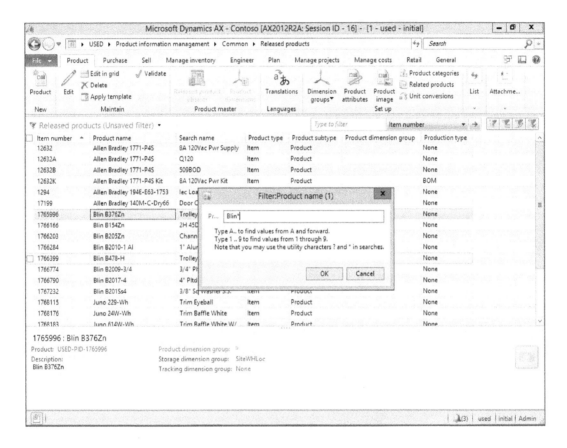

When the Filter dialog box is displayed, just type in the regular search expression that you want to filter with, and then click the OK button.

Use The Filter by Field To Search For Subsets Of Data Within Columns

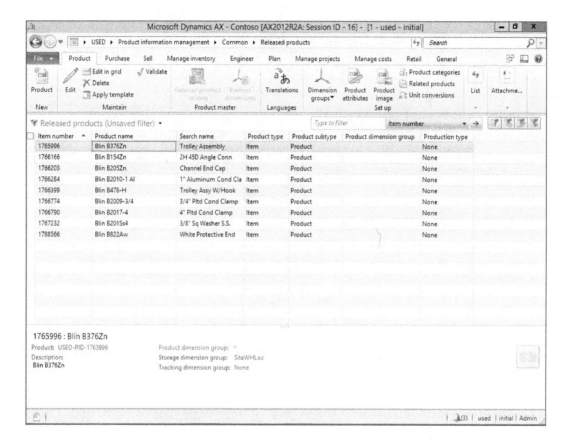

This will refresh the list page, and filter out the data based on the selection that you specified in the search.

That is too easy.

Use The Filter By Grid & Wild Cards To Create More Intricate Queries

Searching and filtering your records based on a field is pretty cool, but in order to hone in on just the right data that you need, you will probably want get a little more creative with your queries, by combining searches, filtering based on ranges, field formats, and value ranges. You will also probably want to filter based on multiple fields at once. Built into all of the list pages is a feature called Filter By Grid that allows you to do exactly that.

No data will be able to hide from you now.

Use The Filter By Grid & Wild Cards To Create More Intricate Queries

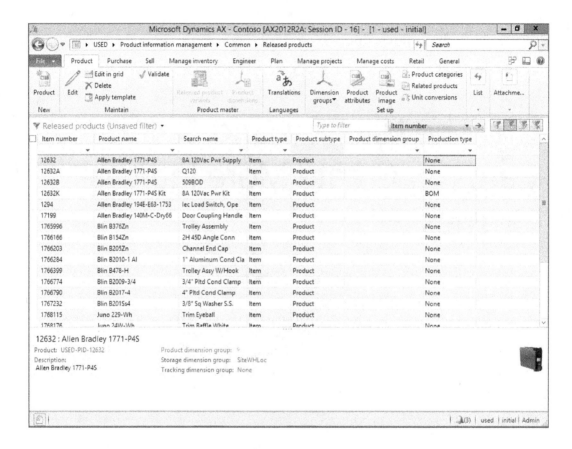

To access the Filter By Grid feature on a list page, either click on the Filter By Grid icon in the title bar of the list page, or press CTRL+G.

This will enable a row at the top of the list page where you can add filters to any of the visible fields. All you need to do is start specifying what you want to search for.

Use The Filter By Grid & Wild Cards To Create More Intricate Queries

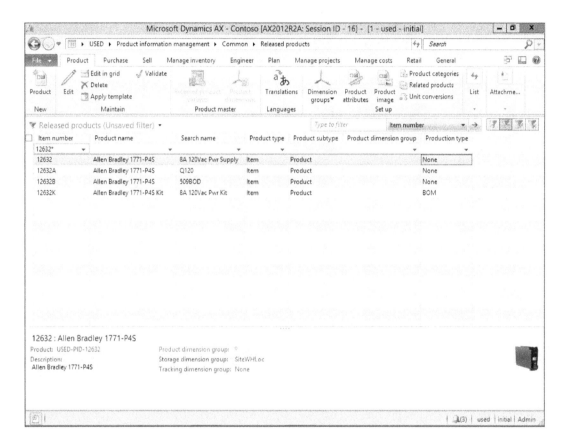

You can use the * qualifier to indicate that any value before or after this point is valid, which is great for searching for records that all start, end, or have the same characters somewhere within the field.

Use The Filter By Grid & Wild Cards To Create More Intricate Queries

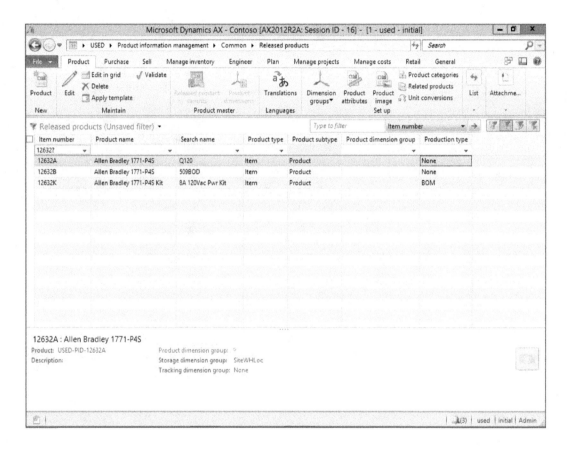

You can use the ? expression to indicate that there must be a character in that spot – you don't care what it is though. This is a great way to select records that are of a certain length.

Use The Filter By Grid & Wild Cards To Create More Intricate Queries

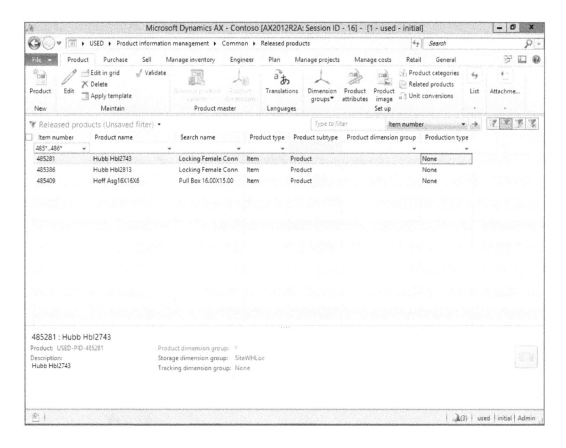

If you want to select a group of records within a range, then you can use the .. expression in the middle of the low and high filters. Note that the low and high values can also be wild carded as well.

Use The Filter By Grid & Wild Cards To Create More Intricate Queries

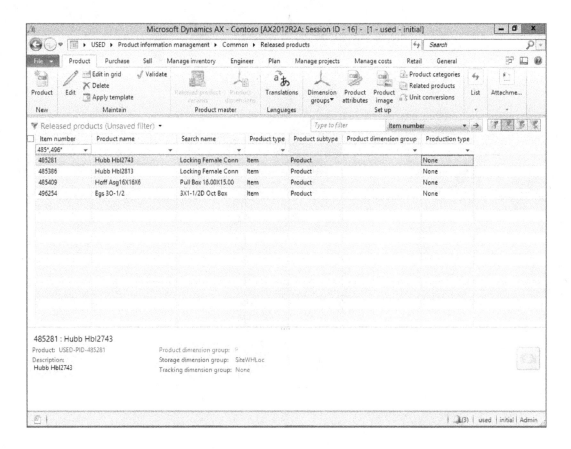

If you want to combine multiple filters together, but not include any values in the middle, then you can append them together by adding a , between them. You can append as many queries together within a field as you like.

Use The Filter By Grid & Wild Cards To Create More Intricate Queries

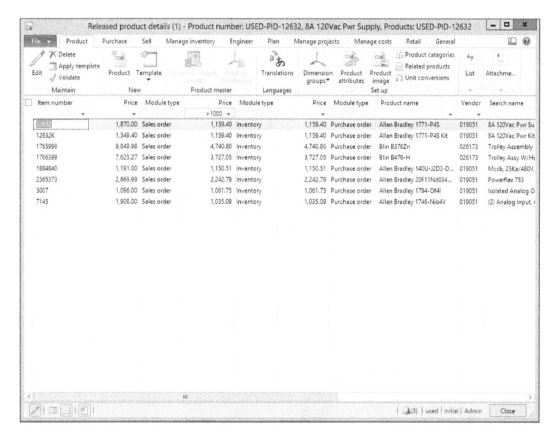

If you have a field that is numeric, then you can use the < and > expressions to select all of the data that is less than or greater than a certain value.

Use The Filter By Grid & Wild Cards To Create More Intricate Queries

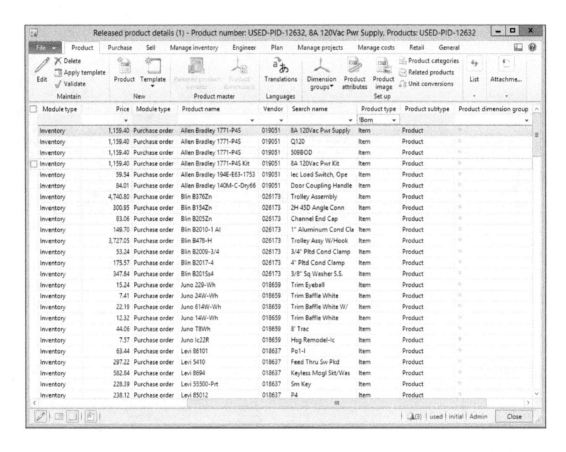

If you want to filter out certain data, then if you add a ! to the beginning of the filter, then you will be saying that you do not want that value. This is a great way to filter out data when there is less that you don't want than you do.

Use The Filter By Grid & Wild Cards To Create More Intricate Queries

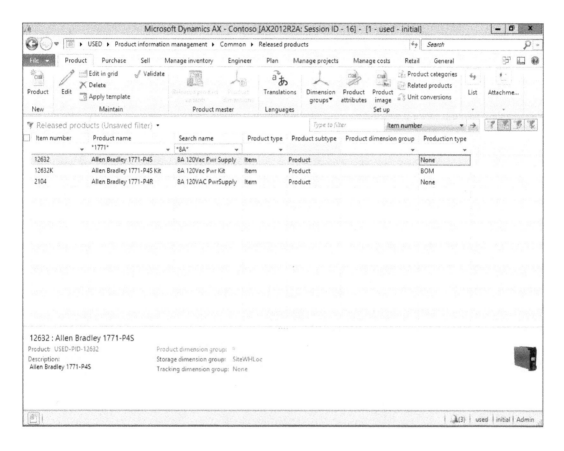

Finally, the most powerful feature of the Filter By Grid option is that you can filter multiple columns at once, creating super filters.

Using The Query Dialog To Create More Advanced Filters

There are a lot of different ways that you can filter out the information in Dynamics AX, but the most flexible one is the Query Dialog. You are probably familiar with this because it shows up a lot when you run updates and reports as the selection box. But you can also access it any time that you are on a list page by pressing CTRL+F3.

This allows you to quickly create custom filters on your data on that is both on the form, and also any additional fields that you may want to add to the query, without having to add additional fields to the form through the personalization. This makes it an incredibly useful way to refine your searches.

Using The Query Dialog To Create More Advanced Filters

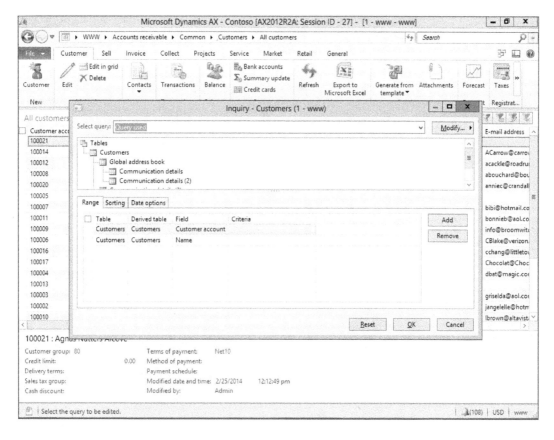

To access the Query Dialog, just press CTRL+F3 while you are on your list page.

When the dialog box is displayed, you will see all of the fields that are being filtered on by default are listed in the Range section.

Using The Query Dialog To Create More Advanced Filters

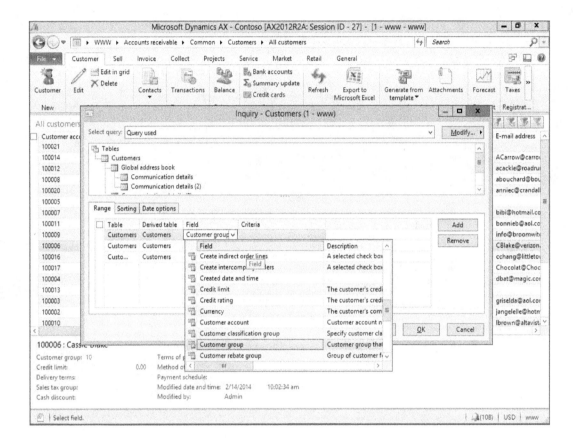

If you click the Add button, then a new range entry will be created, and you can select from any field in the related tables to add as a search criteria.

Using The Query Dialog To Create More Advanced Filters

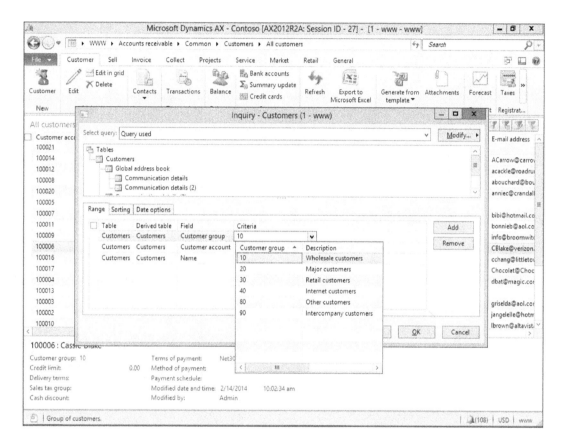

After selecting a field to search on, you can also pull up a list of values for that field to add to your selection criteria.

When you have completed building your query, then you just press the OK button to return to your form.

Using The Query Dialog To Create More Advanced Filters

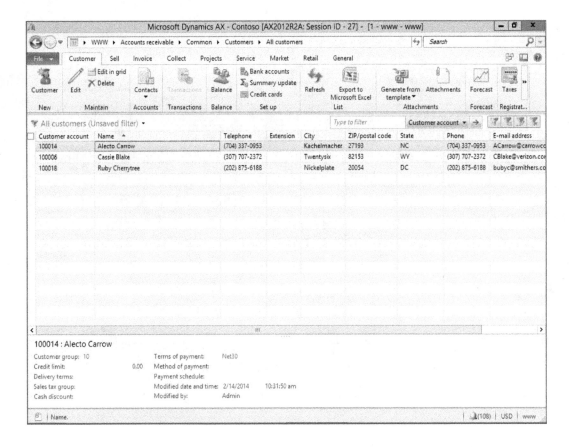

Now you will see that the filter that you built through the Query Dialog has been applied to your form.

FUNCTIONAL TRICKS

There is a lot that you can do functionally within Dynamics AX, but that should just be the starting point. There are a lot of features that are built into the application to support the core functions that allow you to take it to the next level. You just need to know what they are.

In this section we will show how you can use features like Workflow to streamline your approvals, Cases to manage incidents and issues, Print Management to automate document delivery, Portals for collaboration with partners, and also the Registration Forms to simplify production.

Applying Templates To Multiple Products At Once

Product templates are a great timesaver, because they allow you to set up one product, save it's configuration as a template record, and then use it to create new records with those defaults, or apply it to existing records to update the key fields.

If you are updating existing records, you don't have to do them one at a time though, if you select multiple product records, then you can apply the same template to them all in one fell swoop, saving you a lot of time, especially during the data setup phase.

Applying Templates To Multiple Products At Once

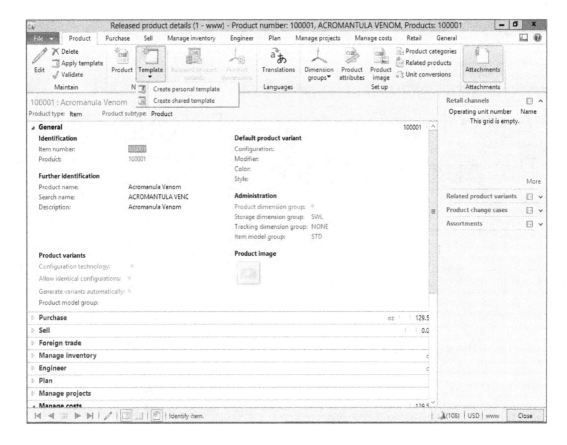

Start off by selecting the product that you want to use as the template and then click on the Template button within the New group of the Product ribbon bar to see the template options. Select the Create personal template option.

Applying Templates To Multiple Products At Once

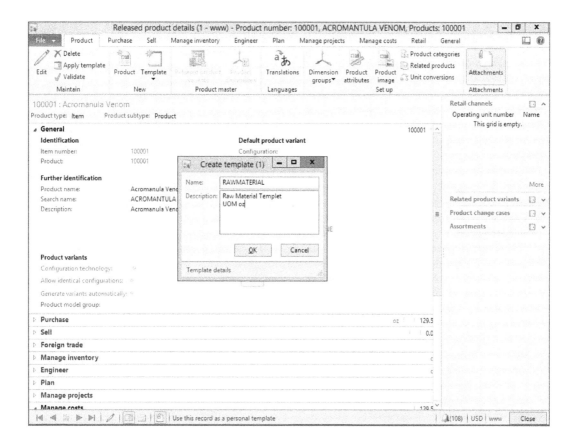

When the Create template dialog box is displayed, give your template a Name and Description and then click the OK button.

Applying Templates To Multiple Products At Once

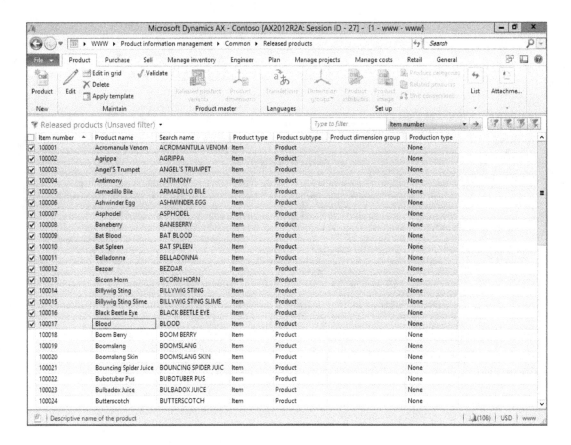

Now return to the Release Products grid view and select all of the products that you want to apply the template to and click on the Apply template button within the Maintain group of the Product ribbon bar.

Applying Templates To Multiple Products At Once

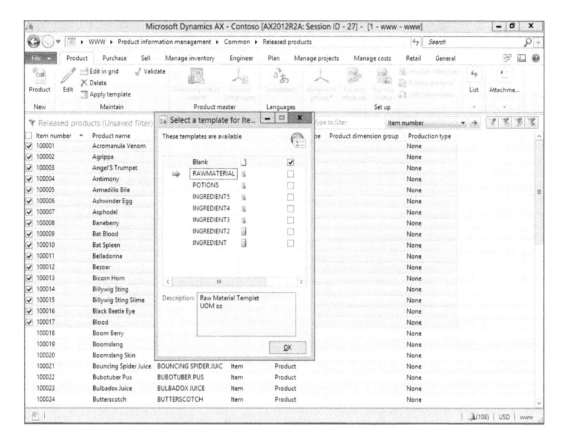

Select your template that you just created, and then click on the OK button.

Applying Templates To Multiple Products At Once

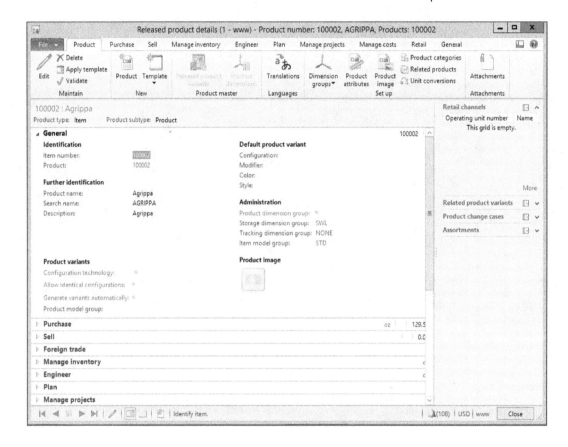

Now all of the products that you applied the templates to will be configured the same way.

Update Product System Templates After They Have Been Created

Product templates are a great time saver because they allow you to use an existing product as a example of how to set up other products, making product setup more of a cookie cutter production line rather than a laborious hand crafting of each record. But as your business changes, you will probably find that you want to update your product templates so that you don't have to continually tweak fields here and there that have changed over time, or maybe you want to remove templates that are now obsolete so that the users don't see them when they are creating new product records.

Don't worry, you can do this directly through the Record Template maintenance form within the Home Area page.

Update Product System Templates After They Have Been Created

Select the Record Templates menu item from within the Setup group of the Home area page.

Update Product System Templates After They Have Been Created

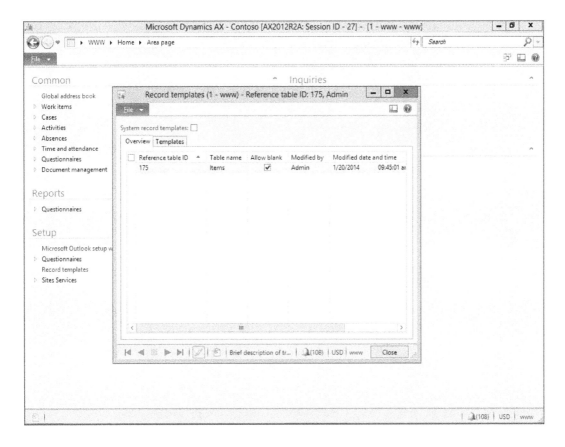

When the Record templates maintenance form is displayed, you will be able to see all of the records that have templates associated with them. In this case we just have templates for the Items.

Update Product System Templates After They Have Been Created

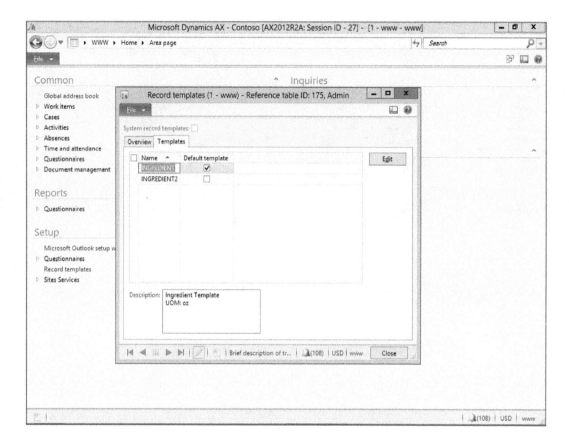

If you click on the Templates tab you will be able to see all of the system templates that you have defined. To change the template, click on the Edit button on the right.

Update Product System Templates After They Have Been Created

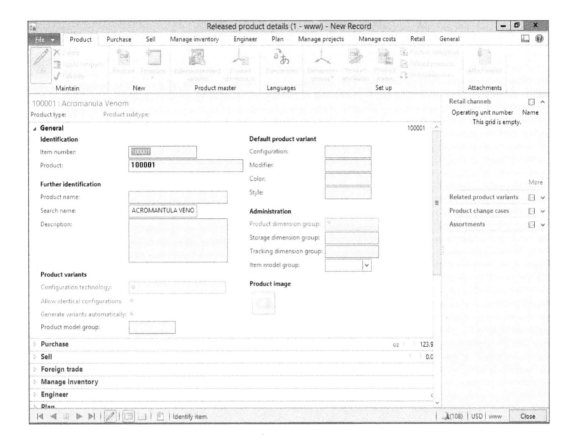

This will open up the Released product that you selected to be the product template, and you can make changes to the key information. Once you have updated the record, click the Close button, and the next time you create a product from that template it will use the new defaults that you defined.

Rename Product Dimensions To Match Your Business

Product Dimensions within Dynamics AX are great because they give you four extra elements that you can use to segregate out all of your products, and you can start reducing the number of base product codes that you use. By default the main three dimensions are named Size, Color, and Style, but if you think of your product dimensions in different terms, don't disregard this feature, because you can rename them to be whatever you like.

Now you can build your product dimensions however you like.

Rename Product Dimensions To Match Your Business

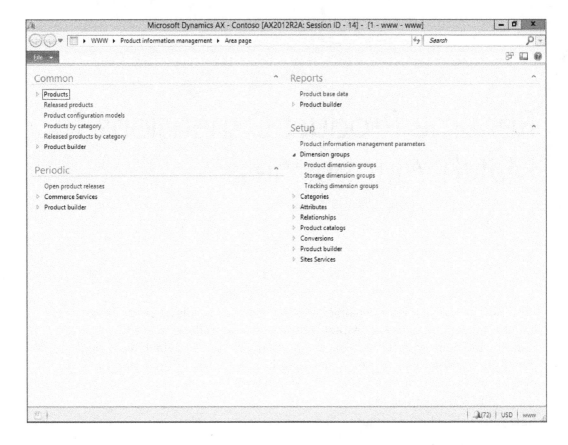

Click on the Product Dimension Groups menu item within the Dimension Groups folder of the Setup group within the Product Information Management area page.

Rename Product Dimensions To Match Your Business

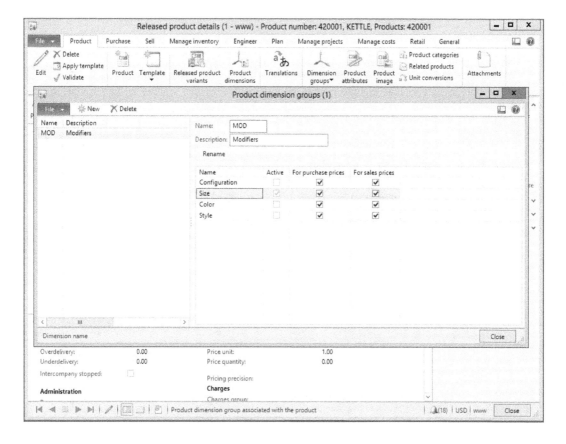

When the Product Dimension Groups maintenance form is displayed, click on any of the records, and then select the Dimension that you want to repurpose. If the dimension is enabled, then the Rename button will become enabled, and you can click on it.

Rename Product Dimensions To Match Your Business

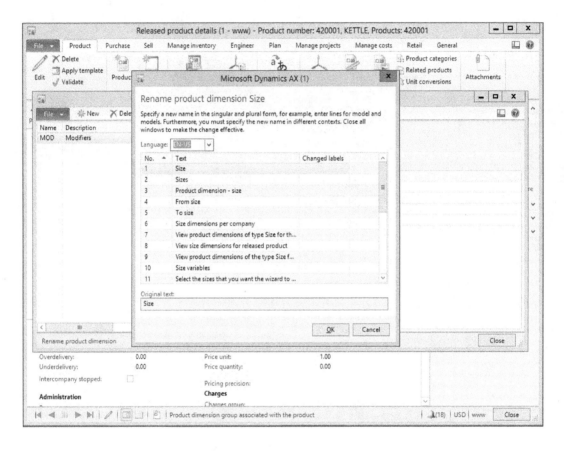

This will open up the Rename Product Dimension Size dialog box. All of the standard text strings will be shown for the dimension.

Rename Product Dimensions To Match Your Business

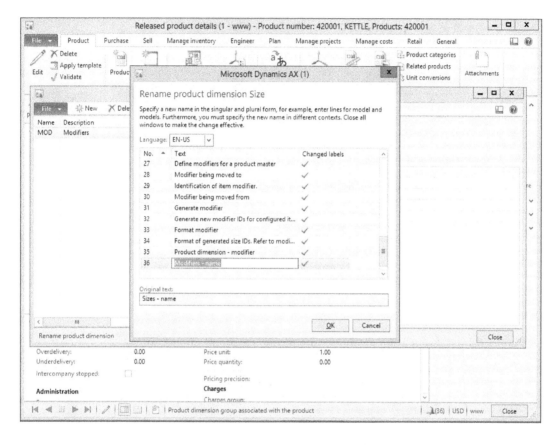

All you need to do is update the standard messages to match the new dimension that you want to track against the products. When you have updated the 36 message files, just click on the OK button to update the dimension.

Rename Product Dimensions To Match Your Business

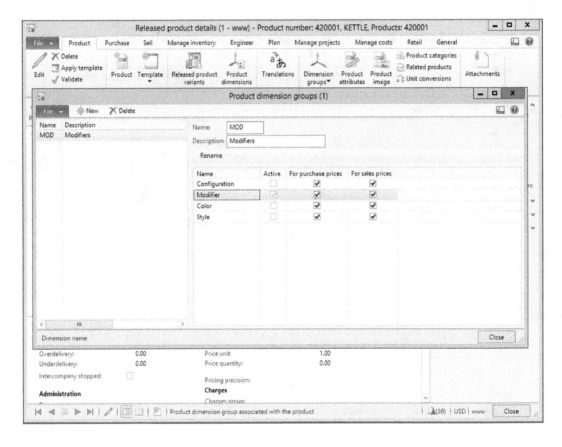

When you return to the Product Dimension Groups maintenance form you should notice that your dimension now uses the new naming convention that you set up.

Rename Product Dimensions To Match Your Business

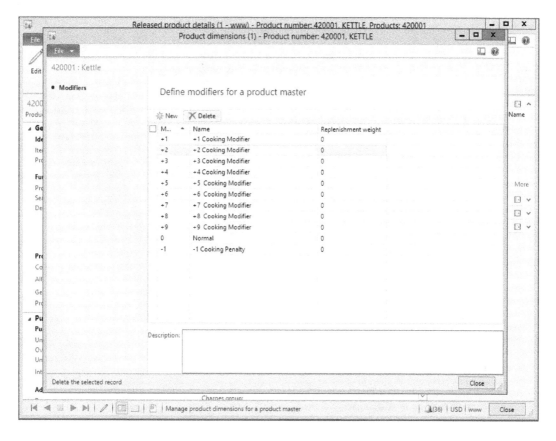

Now when you maintain the valid product dimension values, it will have a new name.

Rename Product Dimensions To Match Your Business

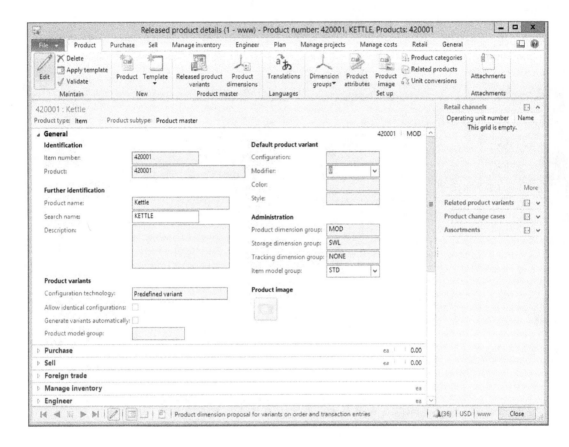

Also, when you look at the dimension within the Released Product maintenance form, it will use the new naming convention.

Rename Product Dimensions To Match Your Business

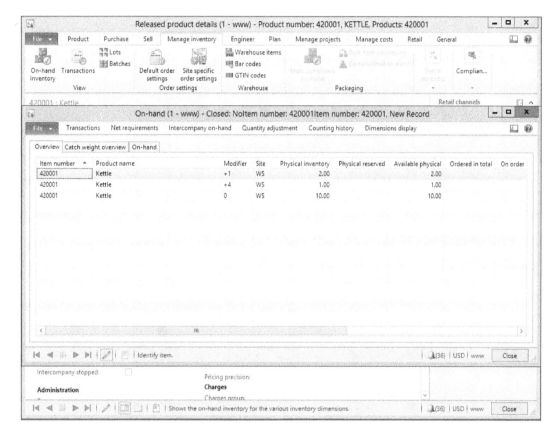

Even the Inventory screens will be changed.

How cool is that!

Manage Your Product Costs By Product Variants

The Product Dimensions are great because they allow you to break out your products into multiple variants based on the rules that you put in place for the product. If those variations are priced and costed differently, then don't worry, there is a quick and easy way to enable costing by variation within Dynamics AX, enabling you to track everything at the product level, but treat them differently based on their configuration.

All products are equal, just some are more equal than others.

Manage Your Product Costs By Product Variants

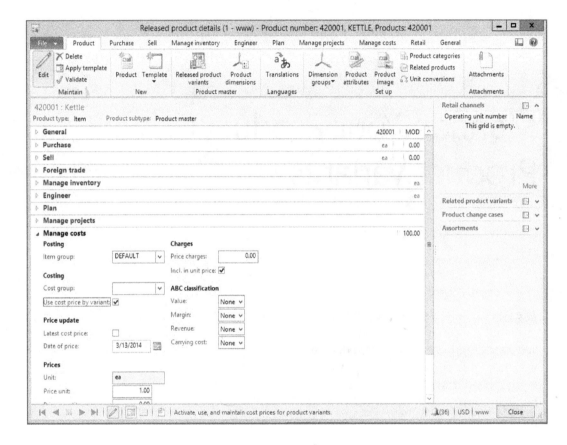

Open up the Released Product record and expand the Manage Costs tab group.

Then check the Use Cost Price By Variant check box.

Manage Your Product Costs By Product Variants

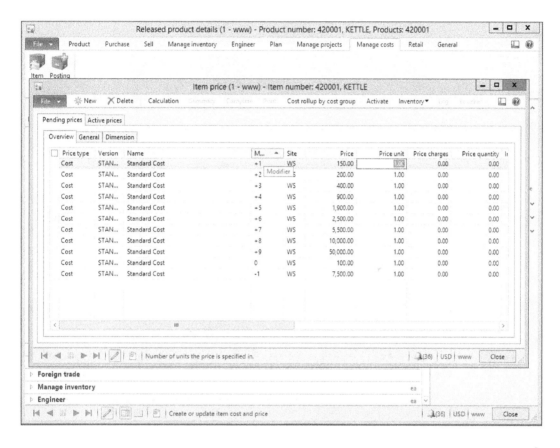

Now when you look at the costs for your Released Product, you will see that the costs are now broken out by the different product variation.

Use Retail Category Attributes To Track Additional Product Characteristics

If you need to track additional characteristics and fields against a product record, you don't have to resort to making a coding change to Dynamics AX. You can add an unlimited number to additional Attributes to a Released Product through the Retail Categories functionality.

Please stop the unnecessary creation of new fields.

Use Retail Category Attributes To Track Additional Product Characteristics

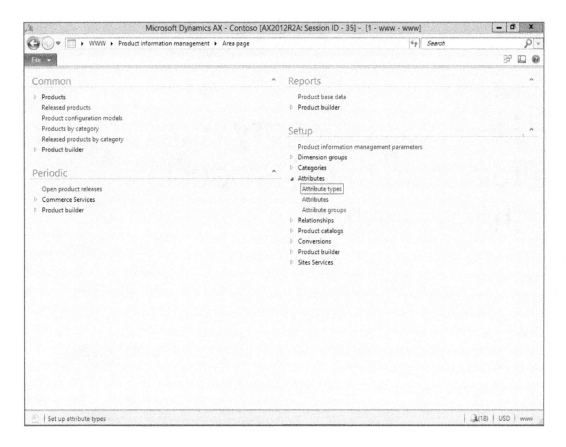

First we need to configure the Attribute Types that we will be using. To do this, click on the Attribute Types menu item within the Attributes folder of the Setup group within the Product Information Management area page.

Use Retail Category Attributes To Track Additional Product Characteristics

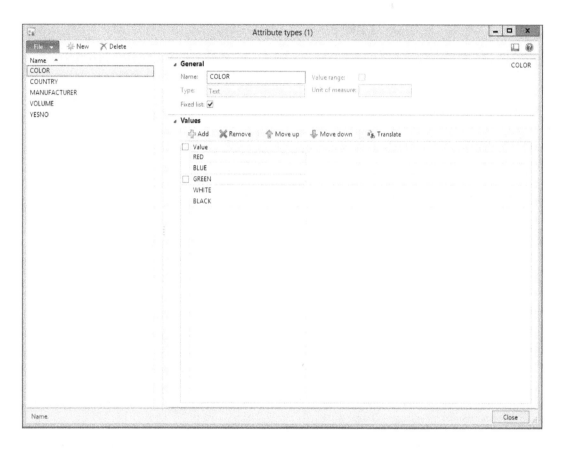

Within the Attribute Types maintenance form, add a new record for each of the different types that you will be using for your attributes.

Use Retail Category Attributes To Track Additional Product Characteristics

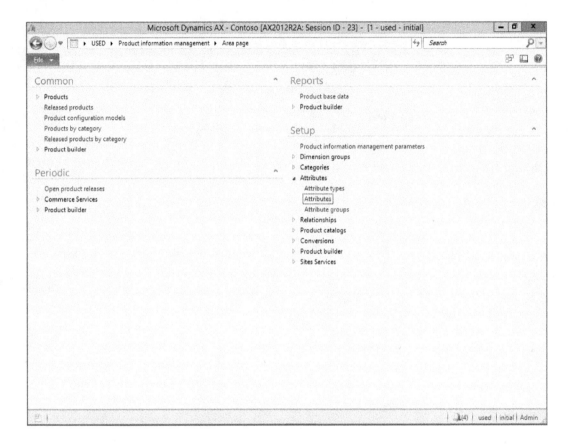

The next step is to configure the Attributes themselves that we will be using. To do this, click on the Attributes menu item within the Attributes folder of the Setup group within the Product Information Management area page.

Use Retail Category Attributes To Track Additional Product Characteristics

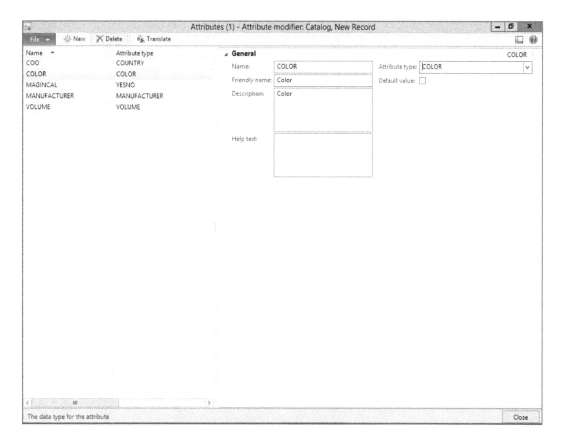

Within the Attributes maintenance form, add a new record for each of the different attribute that you want to track against the products and then link them to the Attribute Type that they will be using.

Use Retail Category Attributes To Track Additional Product Characteristics

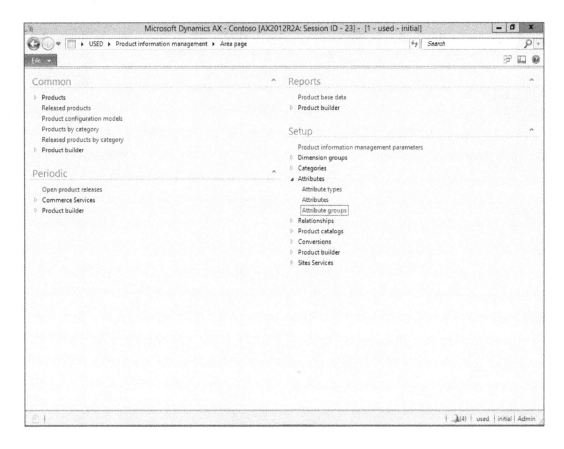

Now we need to configure an Attributes Group that will be used to reference all of the Attributes that we will be using. To do this, click on the Attribute Groups menu item within the Attributes folder of the Setup group within the Product Information Management area page.

Use Retail Category Attributes To Track Additional Product Characteristics

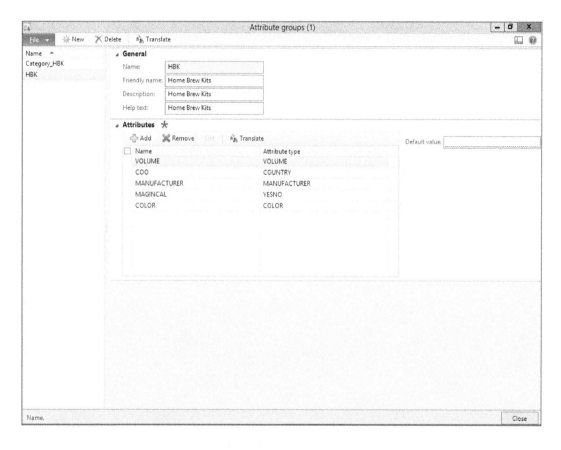

Within the Attribute Groups maintenance form, add a new record for an attribute group and then add all of the Attributes that you want to use within that group.

Use Retail Category Attributes To Track Additional Product Characteristics

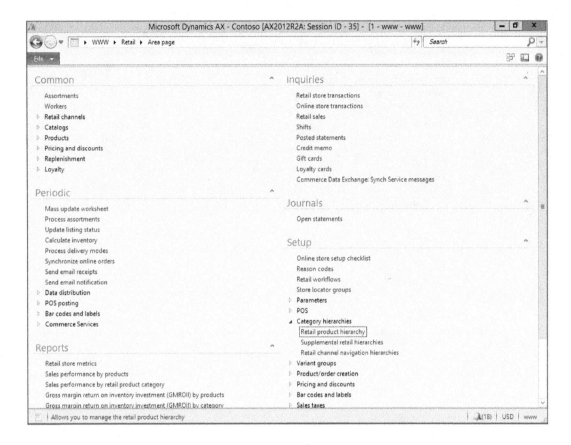

Finally we need to associate the Attribute Group to a Retail Product Hierarchy so that it will default in the Attributes against a product. To do this, click on the Retail Product Hierarchy menu item within the Category Hierarchy folder of the Setup group within the Retail area page.

Use Retail Category Attributes To Track Additional Product Characteristics

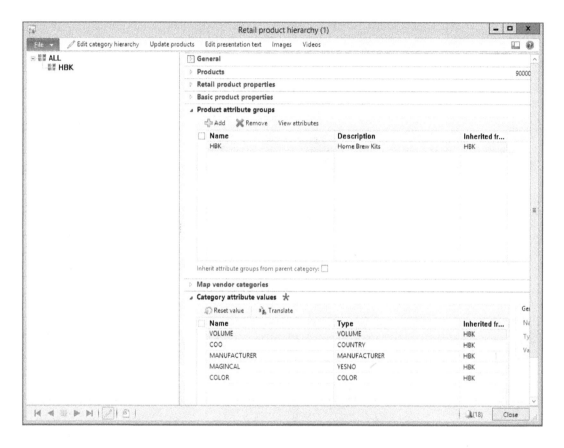

When the Retail Product Hierarchy maintenance form is displayed, click on the node in the hierarchy that you want to inherit the attributes, and add the Attribute Group to the Product Attribute Groups tab.

If you look at the values within the Category Attribute Values tab, then all of the attributes that you assigned to the group will show up there.

Use Retail Category Attributes To Track Additional Product Characteristics

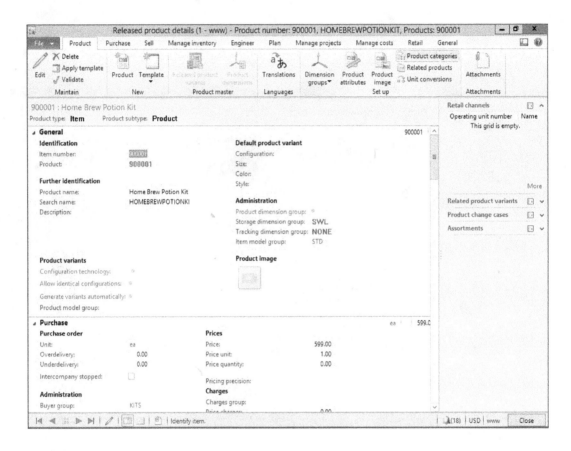

To enable the Attributes against a product all you need to do is have the product assigned to the Retail Category Hierarchy that you configured the Attribute Group against. To do this open up the Released Product and click on the Product Categories menu button within the Setup group of the Product ribbon bar.

Use Retail Category Attributes To Track Additional Product Characteristics

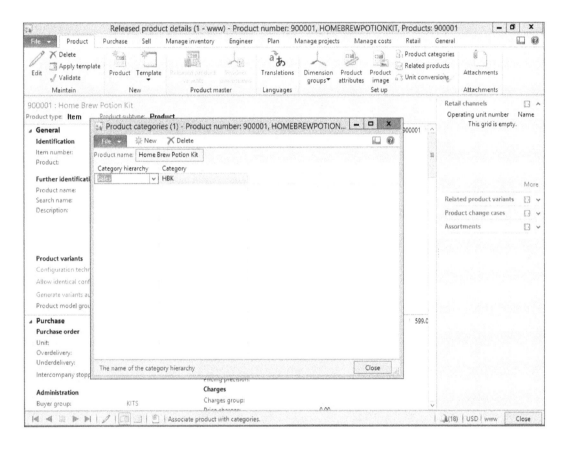

If the Retail category is not associated with the product then just click on the New button in the menu bar to create a new record, and then link the product to the Retail Category.

Use Retail Category Attributes To Track Additional Product Characteristics

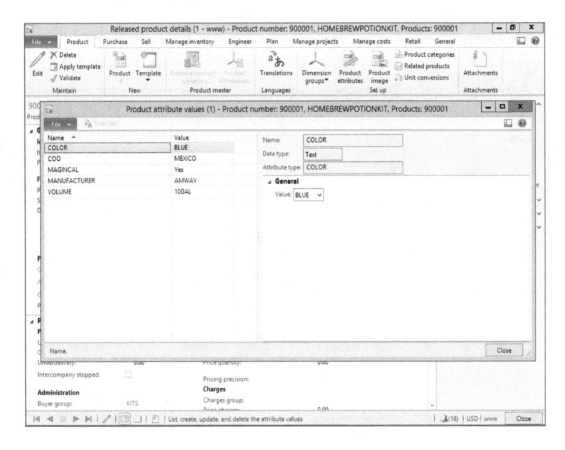

Now when you open up the product and click on the Product Attributes menu button within the Setup group of the Product ribbon bar, you will see all of the attributes are listed and you can maintain the values.

What a great way to track additional field values against a product without any code.

Use Refilling Warehouses To Let MRP Suggest Replenishment Transfers

Dynamics AX allows you to specify warehouses that are designated to refill other warehouses. This feature is really useful because it will make MRP top up the stock within the child warehouses through transfers rather than a purchase order, and then plan to purchase more product at the refilling warehouse to cover the demand. There is also no limit to the number of levels that you can have, so smaller retail locations can be refilled from area distribution centers, which could be replenished from a central production of receiving center.

This makes your purchasing a lot more centralized and stops you from nickel and diming your suppliers with small orders from each location.

Use Refilling Warehouses To Let MRP Suggest Replenishment Transfers

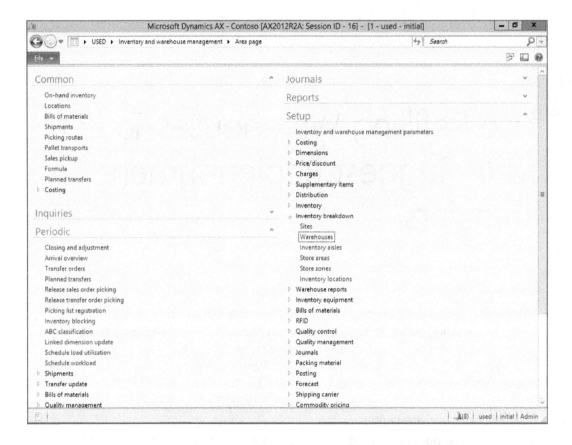

To set up the warehouse refilling policies, just click on the Warehouses link within the Inventory Breakdown folder of the Setup group within the Inventory and Warehouse Management area page.

Use Refilling Warehouses To Let MRP Suggest Replenishment Transfers

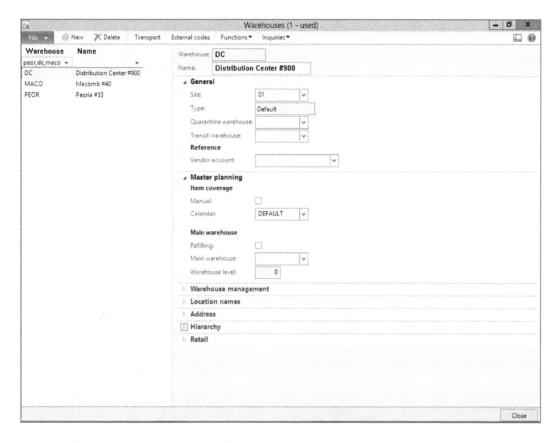

In this example our first warehouse is the centralized purchasing location, so don't check the Refilling option within the Master Planning tab.

Use Refilling Warehouses To Let MRP Suggest Replenishment Transfers

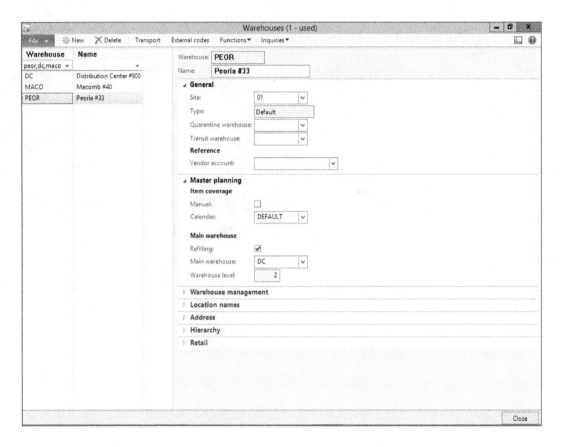

This next warehouse is refilled from the distribution center, so check the Refilling option and set the Main Warehouse to be the parent distribution center warehouse.

Use Refilling Warehouses To Let MRP Suggest Replenishment Transfers

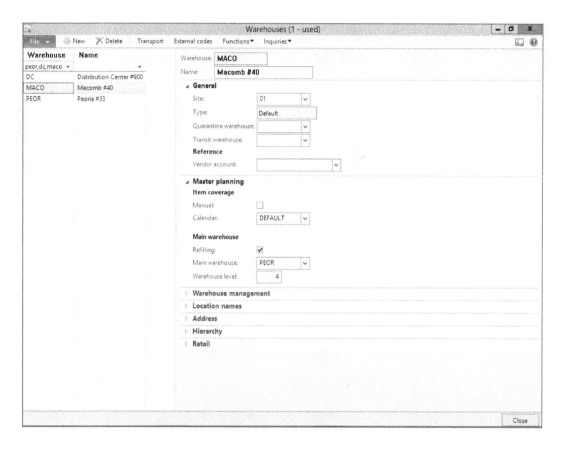

For the final warehouse we will also check the Refilling option but set the Main Warehouse to be the local distribution warehouse.

Use Refilling Warehouses To Let MRP Suggest Replenishment Transfers

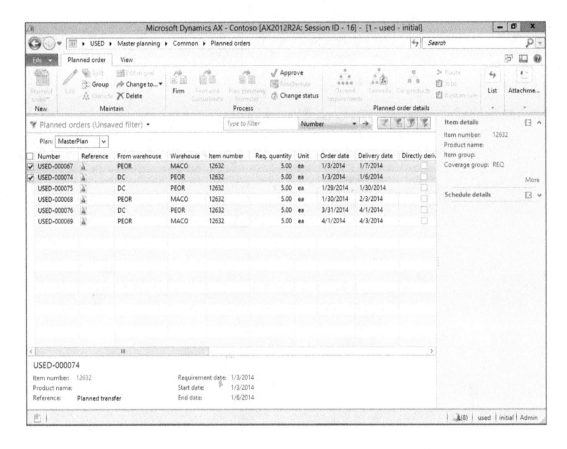

Now when you run your MRP, if you have demand at the child warehouse, then planning will create a transfer from the local distribution center to satisfy it, and that in turn will be replenished from the main warehouse through a transfer as well.

Now you just have to organize for the carriers and you are done.

Configure the Carrier Interface in Test Mode to Record Tracking Numbers Manually

If you want to track parcel shipment tracking numbers within Dynamics AX, but have not got the volume of orders to justify installing the FedEx, or UPS software, then don't worry. You can track this information manually by turning on the Carrier Interfaces, but configuring them to run in test mode.

Configured this way, you will be asked to enter in the tracking information whenever the Packing Slip is created.

Configure the Carrier Interface in Test Mode to Record Tracking Numbers Manually

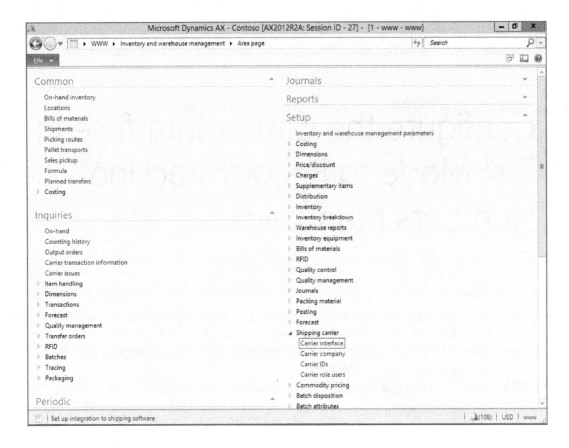

Click on the Carrier Interface menu item within the Shipping Carrier folder of the Setup group within the Inventory and Warehouse Management area page.

Configure the Carrier Interface in Test Mode to Record Tracking Numbers Manually

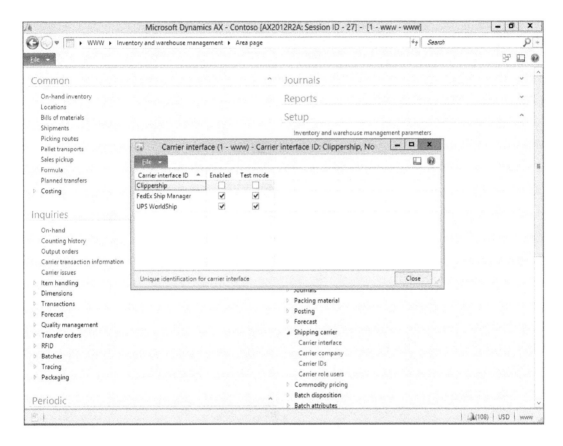

When the Carrier Interface maintenance form is displayed, check the Enabled and Test Mode check boxes for the FedEx and UPS Carrier Interface ID's.

Configure the Carrier Interface in Test Mode to Record Tracking Numbers Manually

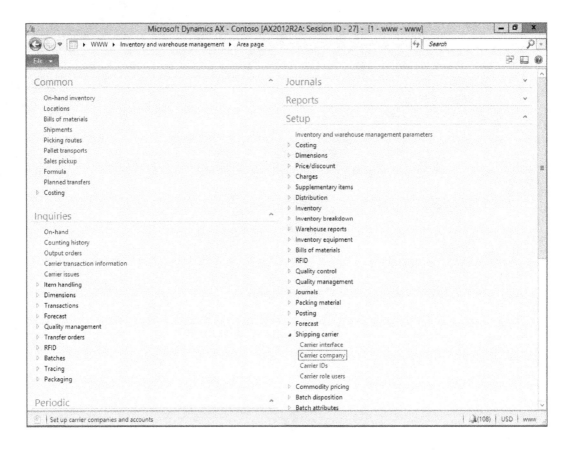

Next, click on the Carrier Company menu item within the Shipping Carrier folder of the Setup group within the Inventory and Warehouse Management area page.

Configure the Carrier Interface in Test Mode to Record Tracking Numbers Manually

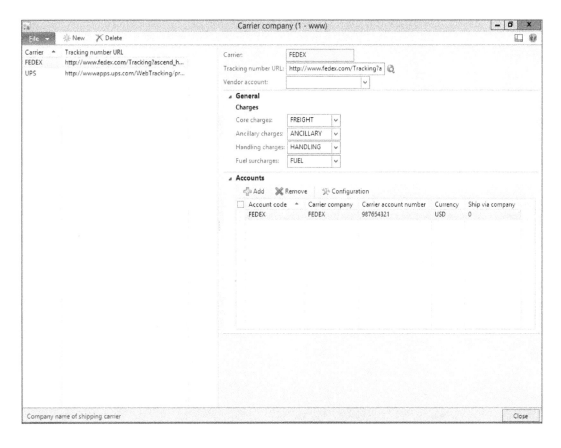

When the Carrier Company maintenance form is displayed, add two new records for FedEx, and UPS.

Note: If you want to configure the tracking number URL links, then here they are:

http://www.fedex.com/Tracking?ascend_header&clienttype=dotcom&cntry_code=us &language=english&trackingnumbers=%1

http://wwwapps.ups.com/WebTracking/processInputRequest?HTMLVersion=5.0&loc= en_US&tracknum=%1

Configure the Carrier Interface in Test Mode to Record Tracking Numbers Manually

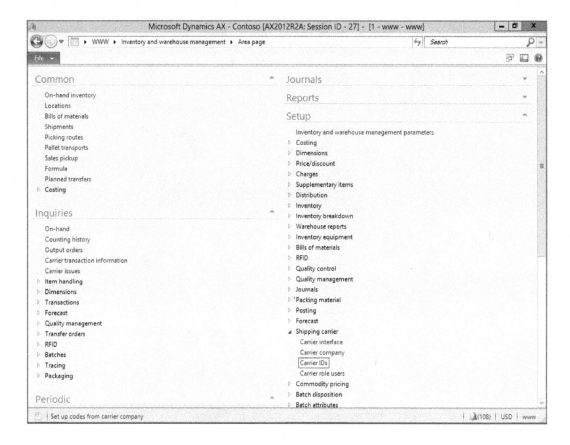

Now, click on the Carrier IDs menu item within the Shipping Carrier folder of the Setup group within the Inventory and Warehouse Management area page.

Configure the Carrier Interface in Test Mode to Record Tracking Numbers Manually

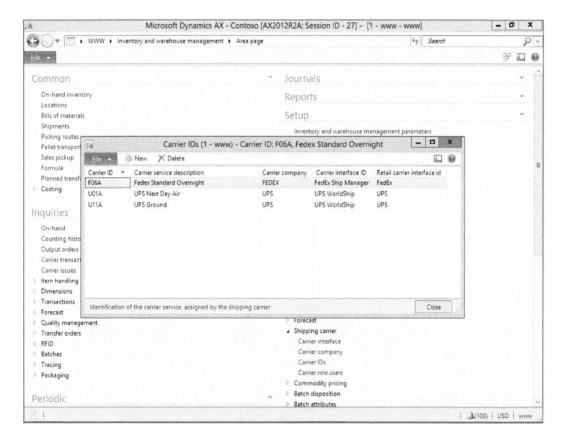

When the Carrier IDs maintenance form is displayed, add records for each of the services that you want to use for each carrier.

Configure the Carrier Interface in Test Mode to Record Tracking Numbers Manually

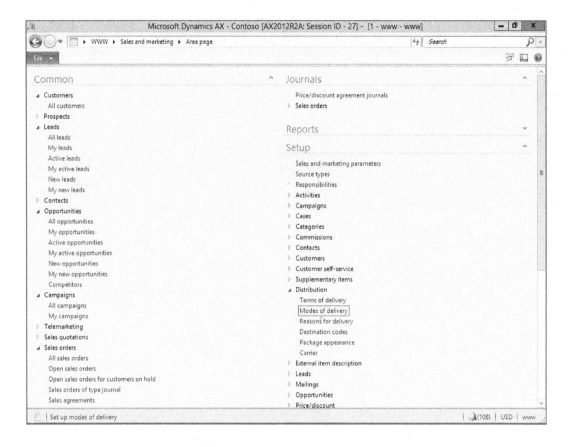

Finally, click on the Modes of Delivery menu item within the Distribution folder of the Setup group within the Sales and Marketing area page.

Configure the Carrier Interface in Test Mode to Record Tracking Numbers Manually

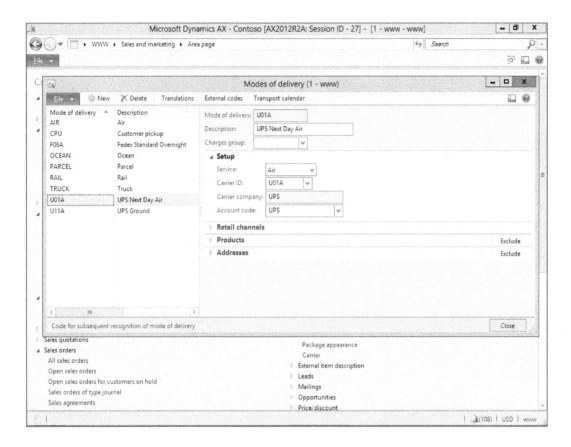

When the Modes of Delivery maintenance form is displayed, you can either create new records for the Carrier Service ID's that you created, or associate them with existing Modes of Delivery to make them the default.

Configure the Carrier Interface in Test Mode to Record Tracking Numbers Manually

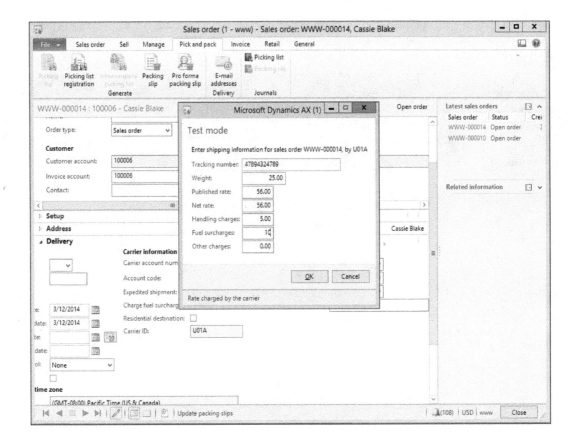

Now when you create a Sales Order that has a Mode of Delivery that has a Carrier Interface associated with it, since this is in test mode, it will ask you to fill in all of the shipping information by hand.

Configure the Carrier Interface in Test Mode to Record Tracking Numbers Manually

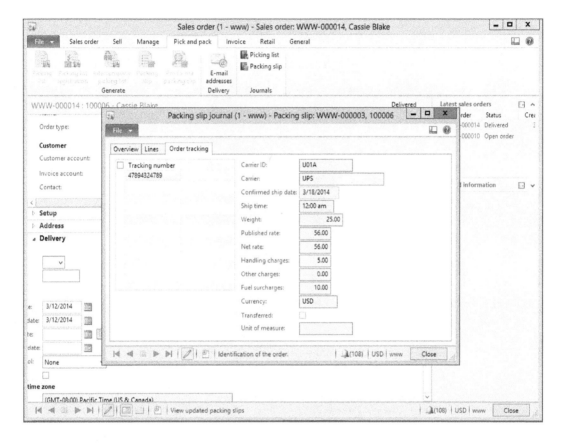

You can then inquire on the Packing Slip Journal at any time and see all of the carrier tracking information.

Configure the Carrier Interface in Test Mode to Record Tracking Numbers Manually

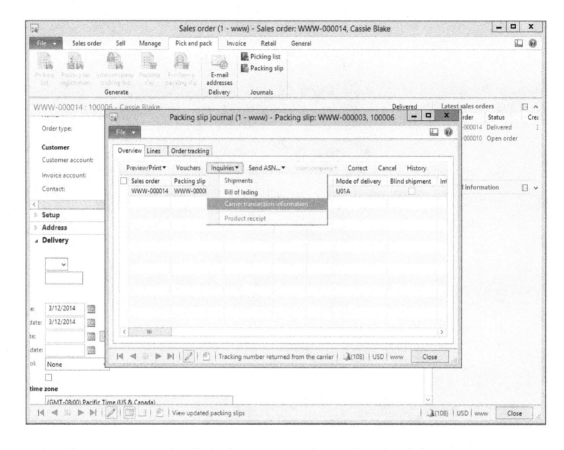

Also, if you want more detailed information on the tracking details for the shipment, click on the Inquiries menu button within the Overview tab of the Packing Slip Journal inquiry form, and select the Carrier Transaction Information option.

Configure the Carrier Interface in Test Mode to Record Tracking Numbers Manually

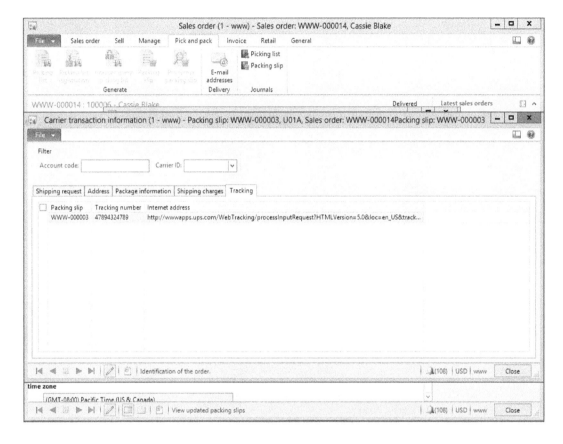

This will show you all of the Tracking Information, and also give you a link to the carriers web tracking portal.

Configure Notes To Print On Standard Forms Like The Order Confirmation

The forms standard forms like the Order Confirmation are a lot more dynamic than you may think. If you have standard notes that you want to include on every document, or if you need to add record specific notes to the header of the lines then they can be configured to pick up the document attachment notes all without a single line of code.

No more sticky notes on your documents.

Configure Notes To Print On Standard Forms Like The Order Confirmation

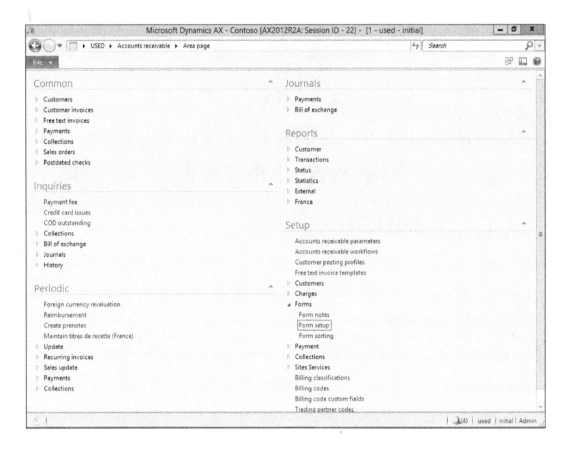

Before we start we need to make sure that the notes are configured to show on the standard documents within Dynamics AX. In order to do this, click on the Form Setup menu item within the Forms folder of the Setup group within the Accounts Receivable area page.

Configure Notes To Print On Standard Forms Like The Order Confirmation

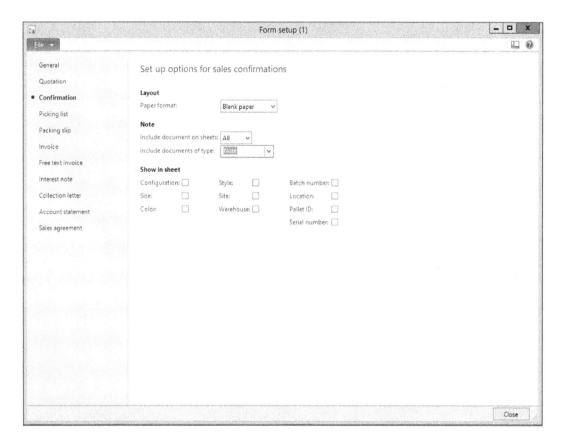

When the Form Setup options are displayed, click on the form that you want to include the notes on.

Configure Notes To Print On Standard Forms Like The Order Confirmation

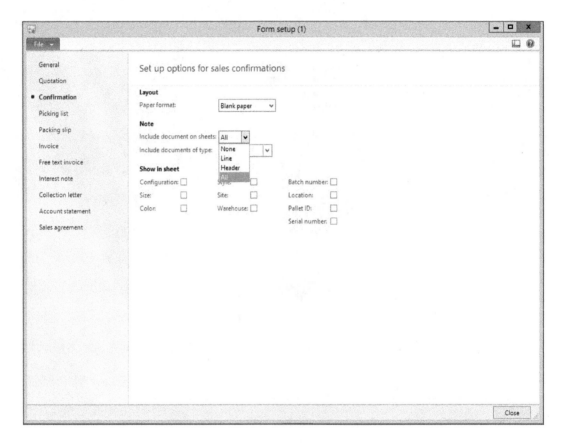

From the dropdown box for the Include documents on sheets field select the locations that you would like the notes to display on.

Configure Notes To Print On Standard Forms Like The Order Confirmation

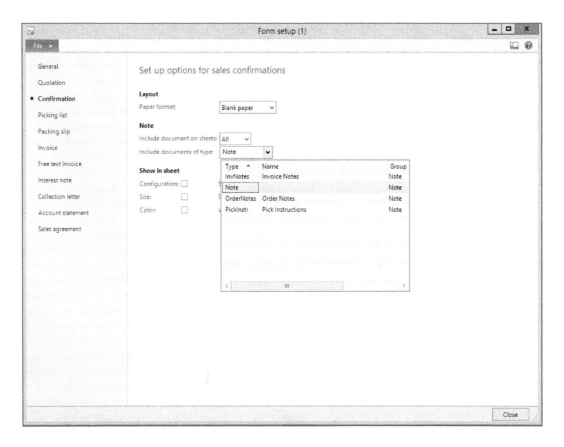

From the dropdown box for the Include documents of type field select the type of note that you would like to display on. You can create additional document types if you like to further differentiate the notes.

When you have done that, just click on the Close button to exit out of the form.

Configure Notes To Print On Standard Forms Like The Order Confirmation

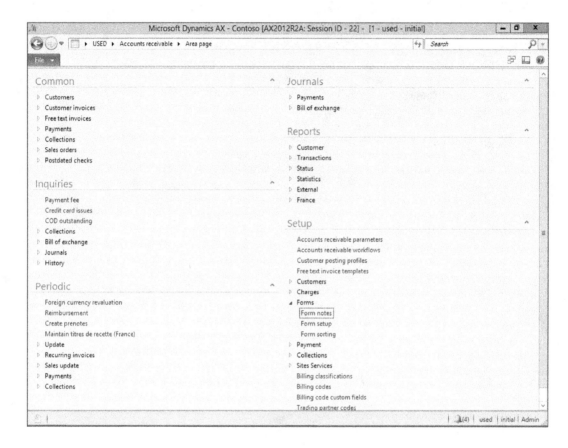

To setup standard notes that display on the documents, click on the Form Notes menu item within the Forms folder of the Setup group within the Accounts Receivable area page.

Configure Notes To Print On Standard Forms Like The Order Confirmation

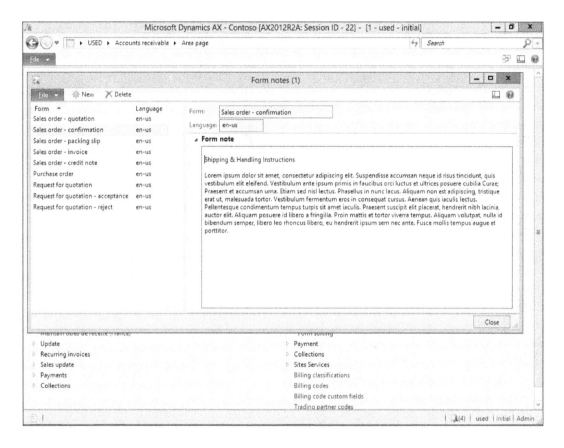

When the Form Notes maintenance form is displayed, you can select the form that you want to add the standard verbiage to and then add the text to the Form Note memo box.

When you have done that, just click on the Close button to exit out of the form.

Configure Notes To Print On Standard Forms Like The Order Confirmation

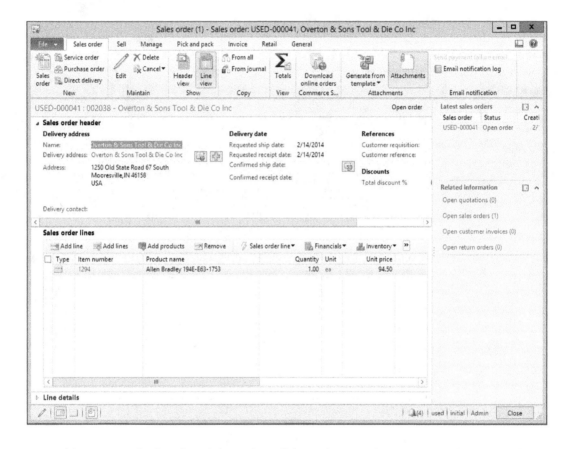

To add a note to the header of the order, click on the Attachments menu button within the Attachments group of the Sales Order tab of the Sales Order record.

Configure Notes To Print On Standard Forms Like The Order Confirmation

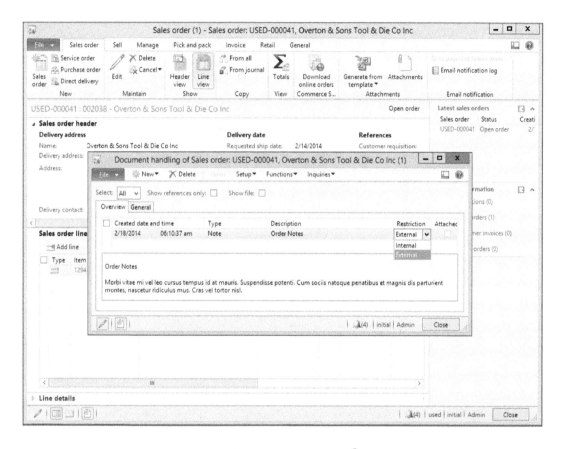

When the Document Handling dialog box is displayed, add a new note with the same Type that you specified in the form setup, add the notes into the body of the attachment, and then set the Restriction field to External.

When you have done that, just click on the Close button to exit out of the form.

Configure Notes To Print On Standard Forms Like The Order Confirmation

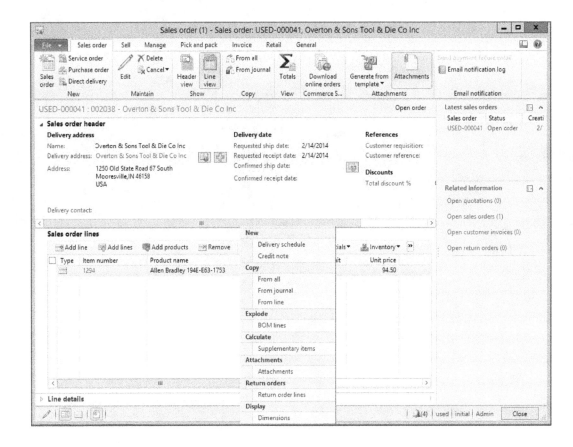

To add a note to the order line, click on the Sales Order Lines menu within the Sales Order Lines group and select the Attachments menu item.

Configure Notes To Print On Standard Forms Like The Order Confirmation

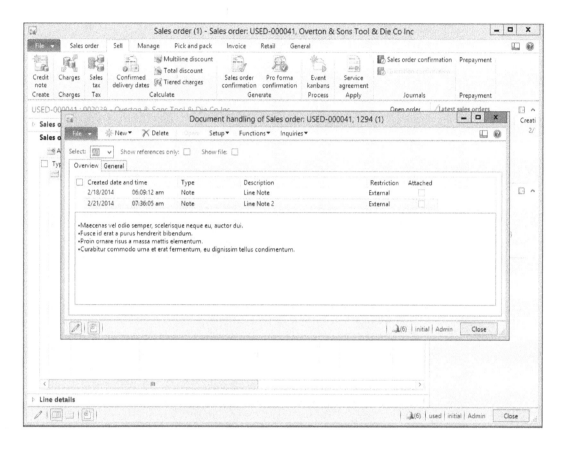

Just as with the header notes, when the Document Handling dialog box is displayed, add a new note with the same Type that you specified in the form setup, add the notes into the body of the attachment, and then set the Restriction field to External.

Note also that you can add as many notes as you like to the line (or header).

When you have done that, just click on the Close button to exit out of the form.

Configure Notes To Print On Standard Forms Like The Order Confirmation

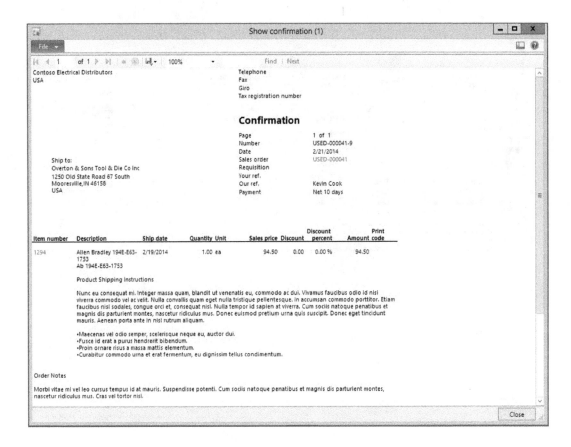

Now when you print out the Order Confirmation, all of your notes will be picked up and printed.

Rock on!

Assign Tasks To Other People Through Activities

You don't have to have all of the CRM functions enabled within Dynamics AX in order to take advantage of some of the features that it offers. You can use features like Activities without any additional setup, which allows you to create appointments, notes, and also tasks.

These activities don't even have to be for you either. If you want to send someone a gentle reminder, then you can create a task, and assign it to anyone in the organization. The task will then show up on their activity list, and also pop up as a reminder in Outlook (if you have the synchronization enabled).

Assign Tasks To Other People Through Activities

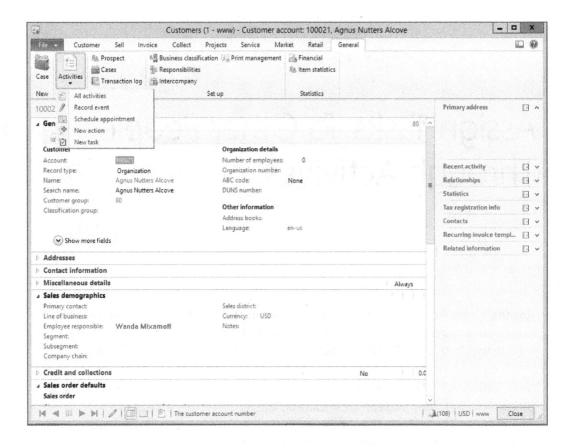

You will usually find the Activities menu button on the General ribbon bar of most of the key record maintenance forms. If you expand the menu you will see all of the different types of Activities that you can track. To create a task, just click on the New task menu item.

Assign Tasks To Other People Through Activities

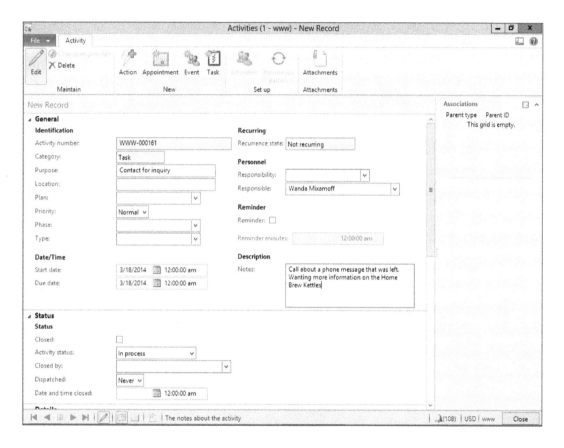

You can give your task a Purpose, a Description, and assign it to a another user by changing the Responsible field.

Assign Tasks To Other People Through Activities

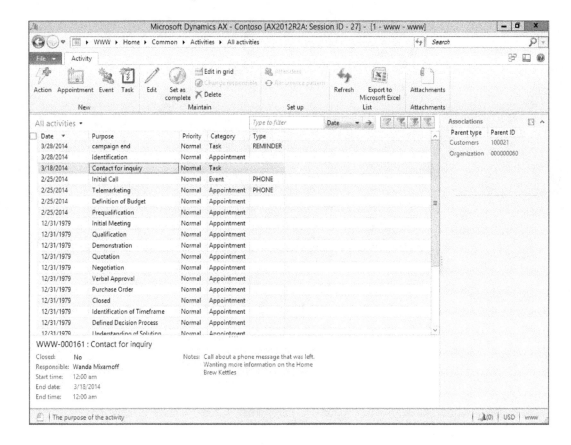

The users are able to see all of the tasks that they have been assigned by opening up the My Activities for from the Activities folder of the Common group of the Home area page.

Creating a Mail Merges In Word From Campaign Target Lists

Sometimes you need to create a more traditional paper mailing for your campaigns, but that doesn't mean that you need to jump through a lot of hoops in order to get it done. The Campaigns function within Dynamics AX 2012 has the ability to create mail merge exports directly from the application that can then be married up to Word mail merge templates. Once you have set this up, your standard mailings are just a matter of clicking a couple of buttons.

Let's keep the USPS in business people.

Creating a Mail Merges In Word From Campaign Target Lists

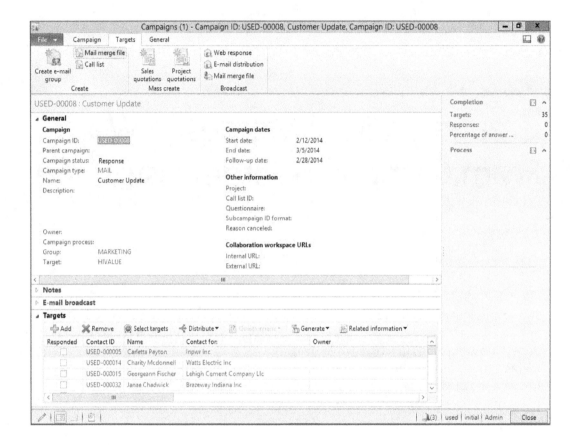

First we need to create a mail merge source file. To do this open up your Campaign with all of the targets selected, and click on the Mail Merge File menu button within the Create group of the Targets tab.

Creating a Mail Merges In Word From Campaign Target Lists

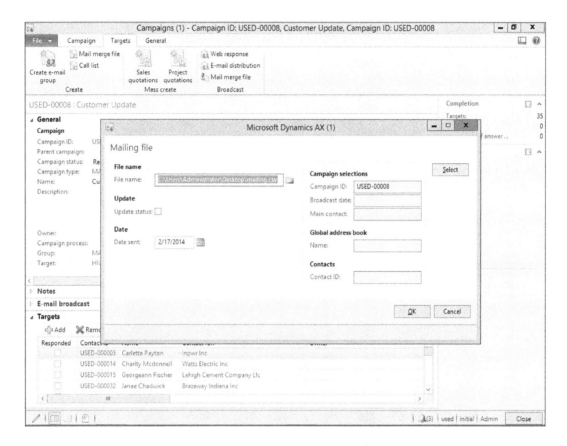

When the Mailing File dialog box is displayed, specify a file path for a .csv file that you will be using to store all of your mail merge data within, and then click the OK button.

Creating a Mail Merges In Word From Campaign Target Lists

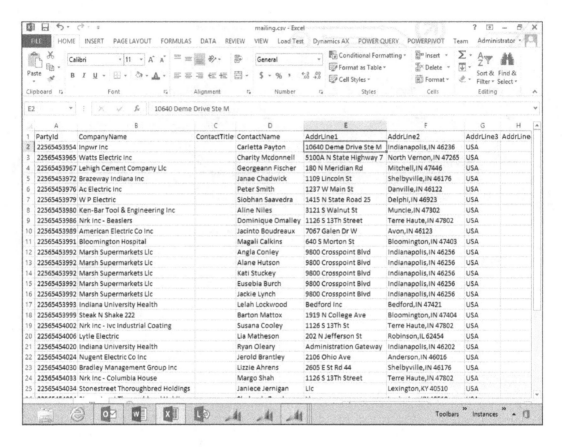

When you open up the .csv file, you will see that all of the contact information for the Campaign Targets will be there and formatted for you.

Creating a Mail Merges In Word From Campaign Target Lists

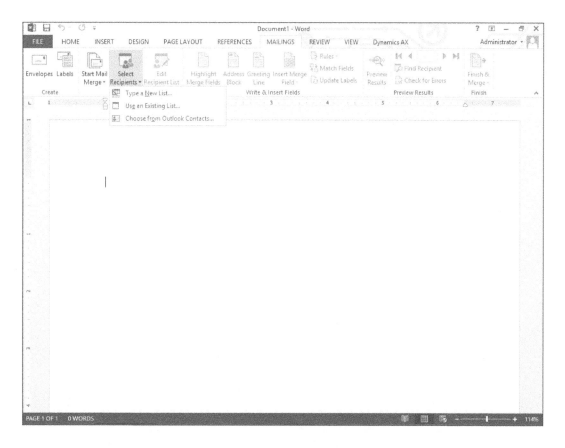

Now we will want to create a mail merge template that we will use as the basis for our campaign mail merge. To do this, open up Word, and select the Use an Existing List menu item from the Select Recipients button within the Create Mail Merge group of the MAILINGS ribbon bar.

Creating a Mail Merges In Word From Campaign Target Lists

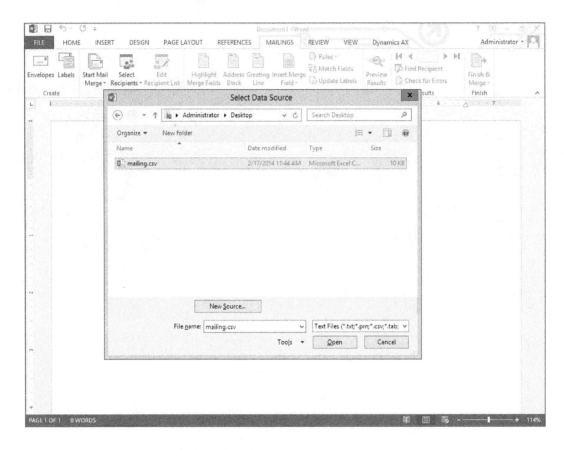

Then select the mail merge file that was created in the previous step.

Creating a Mail Merges In Word From Campaign Target Lists

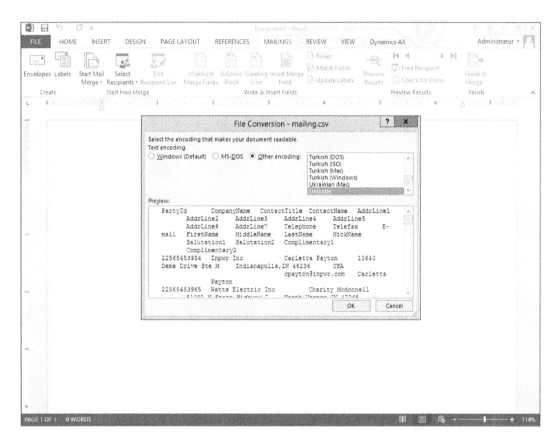

When the File Conversion dialog box is displayed, just select the Other Encodings option, and click the OK button.

Creating a Mail Merges In Word From Campaign Target Lists

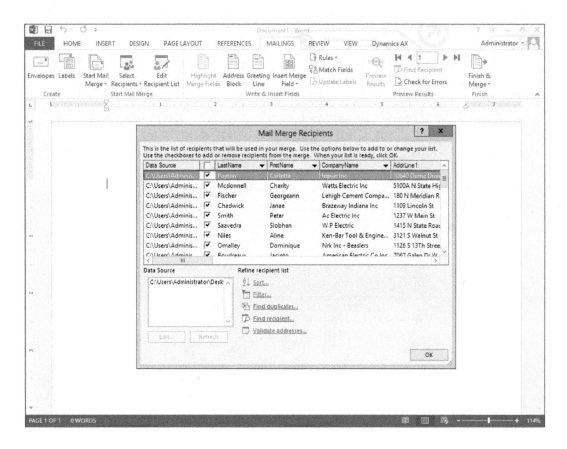

To check that the file has been read correctly, click on the Edit Recipient List button within the Start Mail Merge group of the MAILINGS ribbon bar and you should be able to see all of the records that were transferred from the campaign.

Creating a Mail Merges In Word From Campaign Target Lists

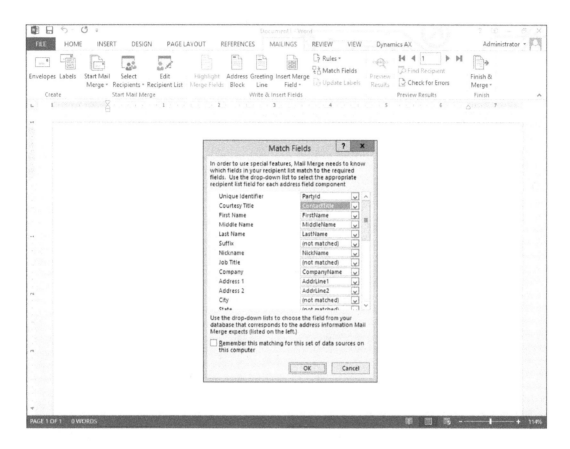

If this is the first time that you are doing this, then you may also have to click on the Match Fields button within the Write & Insert Fields group of the MAILINGS ribbon bar and make sure that all of the fields from the campaign match up to the ones that Word are expecting.

Creating a Mail Merges In Word From Campaign Target Lists

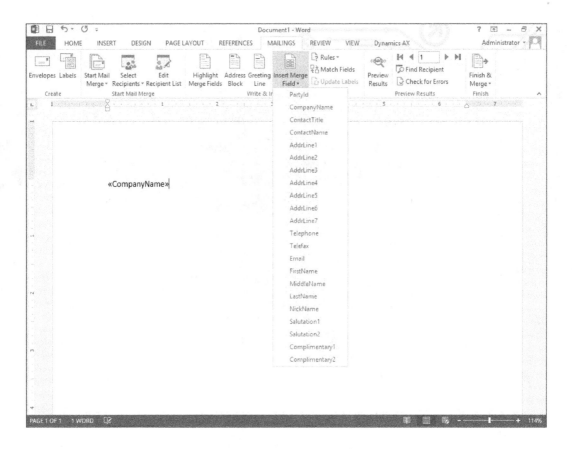

Now all you need to do is select the fields from the Insert Merge Fields button within the Write & Insert Fields group of the MAILINGS ribbon bar and add them to the document.

Creating a Mail Merges In Word From Campaign Target Lists

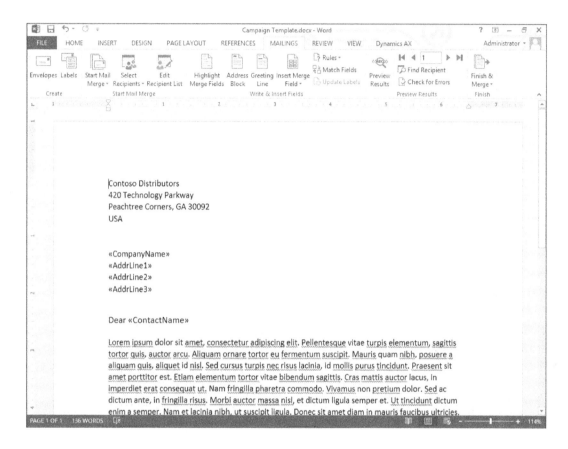

After you have created your mailing, save the template mail merge document.

Creating a Mail Merges In Word From Campaign Target Lists

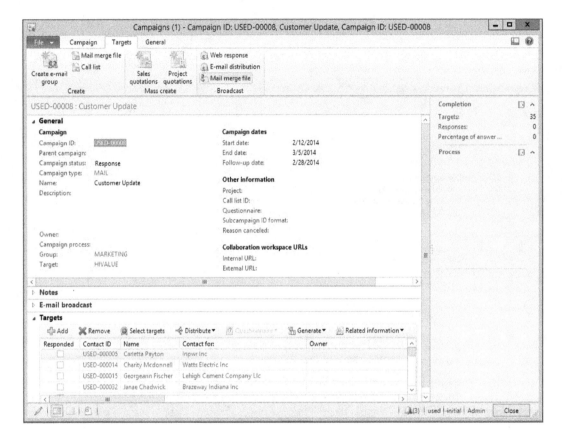

To perform the mail merge, click on the Mail Merge File button within the Broadcast group of the Targets ribbon bar of the Campaign maintenance form.

Creating a Mail Merges In Word From Campaign Target Lists

This will show you a list of all your extracts for the Campaign. Find the extract that you want to use and then paste in the path of the Word template mail merge file that you created.

To link the data with the template, just click on the Template File button.

Creating a Mail Merges In Word From Campaign Target Lists

This will open up the template file and you can click on the Edit Individual Documents link under the Finish & Merge button within the Finish group of the MAILINGS ribbon bar.

Creating a Mail Merges In Word From Campaign Target Lists

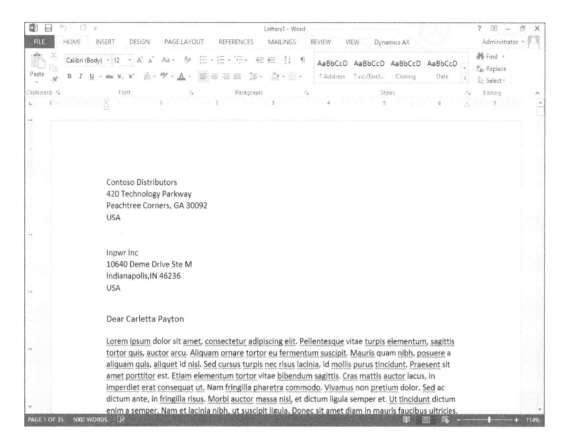

This will create all of your merged files for you incorporating all of the data from the campaign.

Rock On!

Send Personalized Emails To Contacts Through Campaigns

The Campaigns feature within Dynamics AX is a great way to plan & manage marketing projects, but it is also a great way to market to your prospects and customers as well. Once you create your campaign, you can broadcast it through traditional methods like snail mail, or through e-mail blasts with the click of the button.

Getting the word out has never been so easy.

Send Personalized Emails To Contacts Through Campaigns

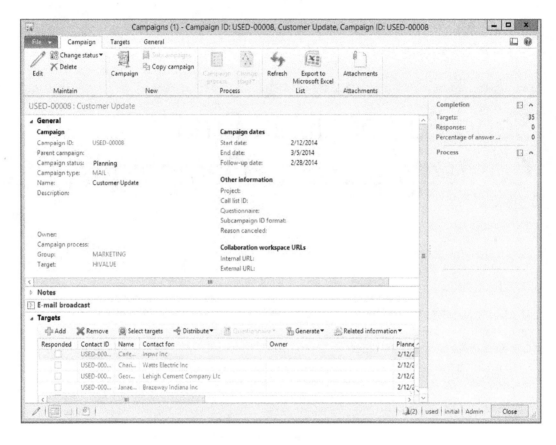

Start off by creating a campaign, and then assigning your target recipients to it.

Send Personalized Emails To Contacts Through Campaigns

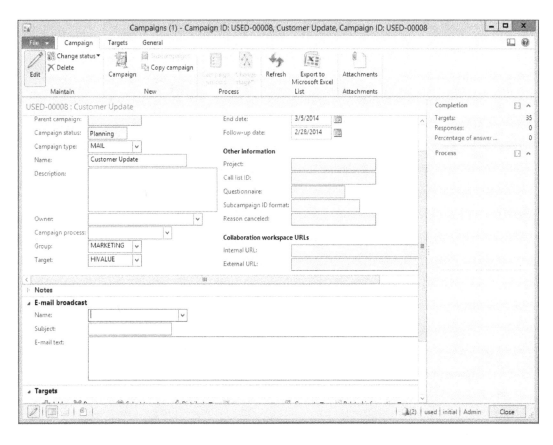

Next, open up the Email Broadcast tab within the Campaign, and select a email template Name.

Send Personalized Emails To Contacts Through Campaigns

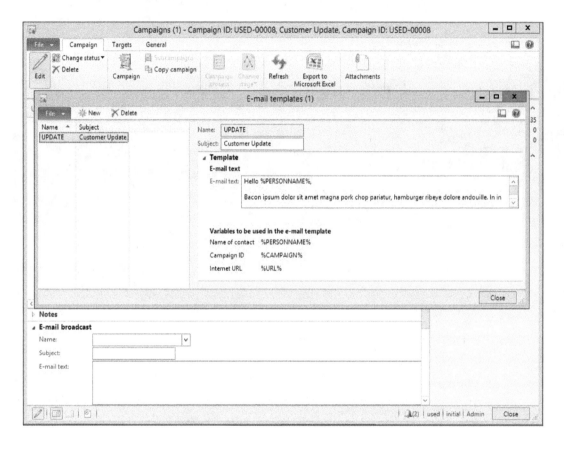

If you don't have an e-mail template created, then just create a new one that has a Subject and a Body. Remember that you can use the email template placeholders to add in personal information from the Contact and Campaign record.

Send Personalized Emails To Contacts Through Campaigns

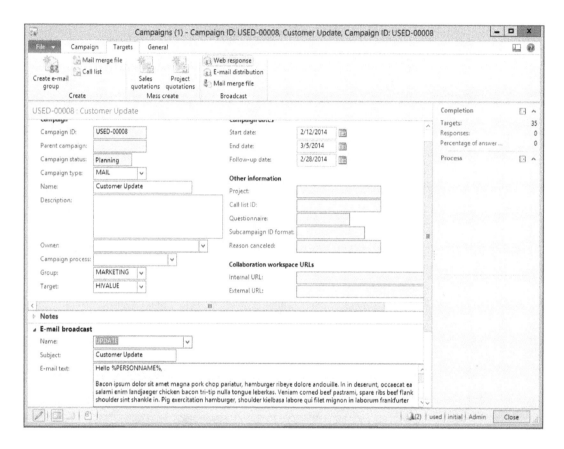

Once you have selected the Email Template the Subject and E-mail Text will populate themselves.

To send an e-mail blast to all of the targets within your Campaign just click on the Web Responses menu item within the Broadcast group of the Targets ribbon bar.

Send Personalized Emails To Contacts Through Campaigns

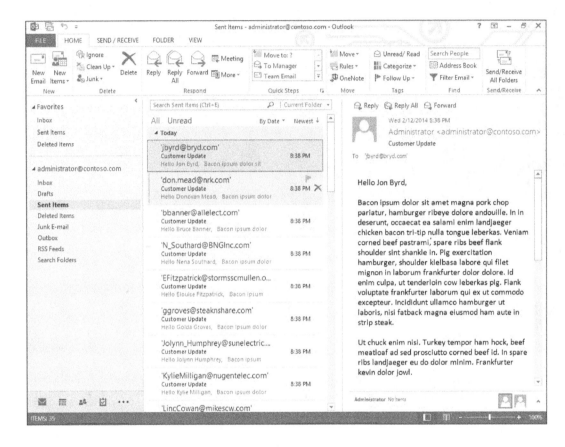

When you check your outbox, then you will see all of the personalized emails.

How easy is that!

Creating Request For Quotations During The Requisitioning Process

The good thing about requisitions is that the users are able to ask for almost anything, although when they ask for something that you have never purchased before, someone has to source it. Dynamics AX makes this a lot easier, because you are able to create a Request For Quotation for any of the requisitioned lines directly from the Requisition itself that then automatically updates the requisition lines when a vendor quote has been approved.

No more off line quoting and manually tracking vendor quotes.

Creating Request For Quotations During The Requisitioning Process

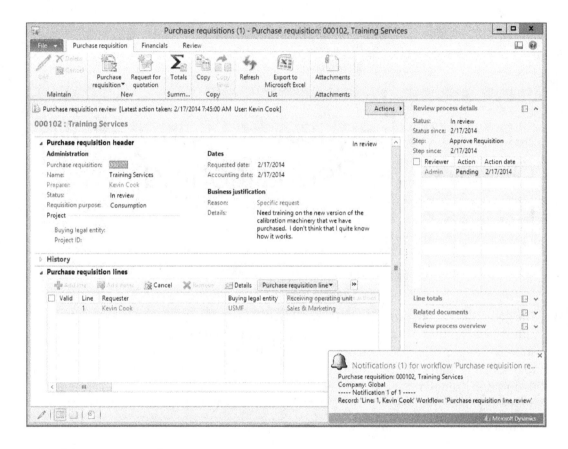

To create a Request For Quotation from a Requisition, click on the Request For Quotation button within the New group of the Purchase Requisition ribbon bar of the Purchase Requisitions form when it is assigned to you.

Creating Request For Quotations During The Requisitioning Process

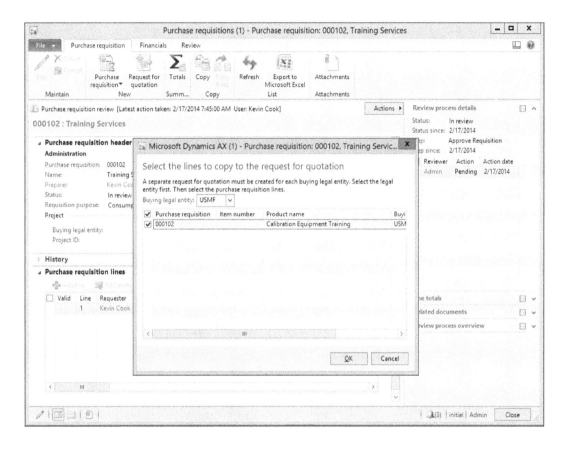

This will open up a dialog box where you can select the lines that you want to submit for Request For Quote. After selecting all the lines that you want to convert to a RFQ click on the OK button to exit from the form.

Creating Request For Quotations During The Requisitioning Process

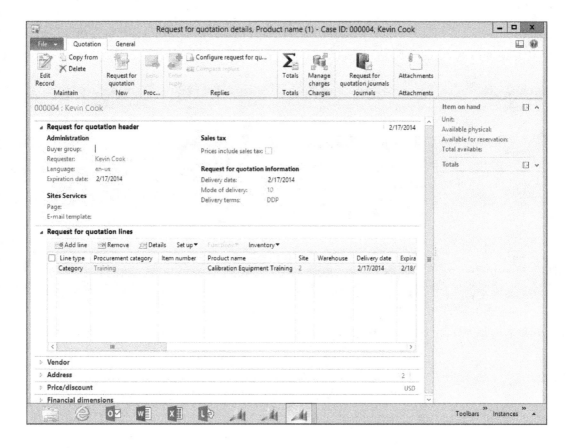

When you open up the Request For Quotations form, you will now see that a new Request For Quotation has been created with all of the lines from the requisition already populated for you.

Creating Request For Quotations During The Requisitioning Process

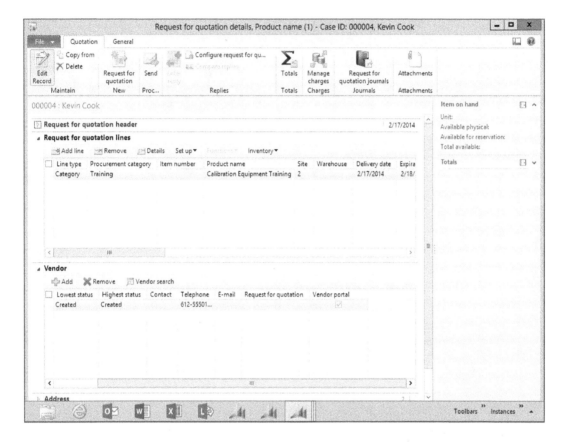

Just add the vendors that you want to request the quotation from within the Vendor tab and then click on the Send button within the Processing group of the Quotation ribbon bar.

Creating Request For Quotations During The Requisitioning Process

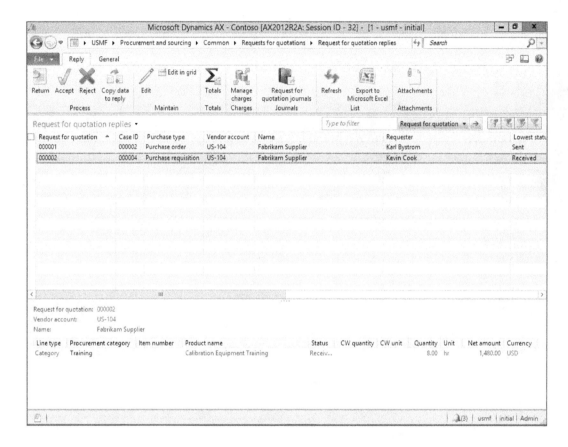

Then it's a matter of waiting for the Vendor to respond to your Request For Quotation (hopefully they will be able to use the on-line Vendor Portal) and if you want to use the quoted values in your Requisition, just click on the Accept button within the Process group of the Reply ribbon bar.

Creating Request For Quotations During The Requisitioning Process

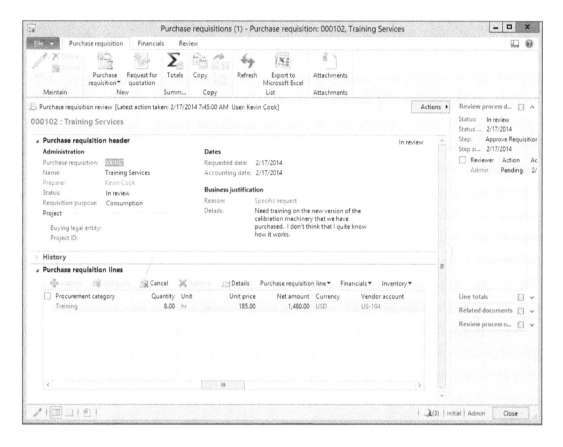

When you return to the Requisition, the quoted values from the Request For Quotation will be automatically updated within the Requisition Lines and also the Vendor will be assigned as well.

All you need to do now is approve the Requisition and then convert it to a Purchase Order.

How easy is that.

Track Skills And Education Against Everyone To Help Match People To Jobs

If you are always searching for people with certain job skills or education for those more specialized jobs, then why not track the Skills and Education levels Dynamics AX. You can track this personal information not only against employees and workers, but also any contact that you have within the system. Then you can use the Skill Mapping functions to find matches.

Consider this tool your own personal recruiter.

Track Skills And Education Against Everyone To Help Match People To Jobs

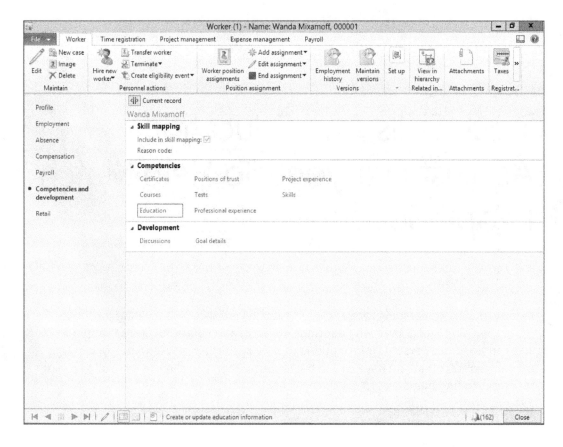

In order to search for people based on their skills and education, you need to first make sure that you are tracking that information.

To update the Education levels against Employees and Workers, open up the record, select the Competencies and Development tab, and then click on the Education link within the Competencies group.

Track Skills And Education Against Everyone To Help Match People To Jobs

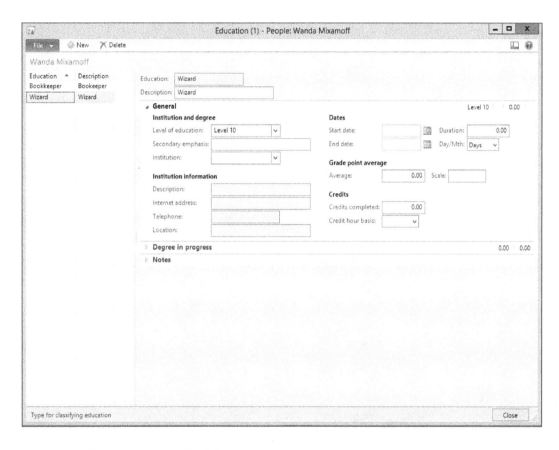

This will allow you to add all of the Education levels that are associated with the worker.

Track Skills And Education Against Everyone To Help Match People To Jobs

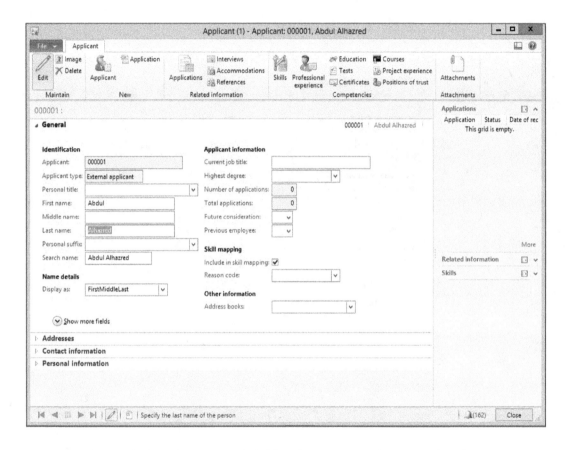

You can also track the Education and Skill levels against Applicants within the HR module as well. To do this, open up the Applicant record, and then click on the Education button within the Competencies group of the Applicant ribbon bar.

Track Skills And Education Against Everyone To Help Match People To Jobs

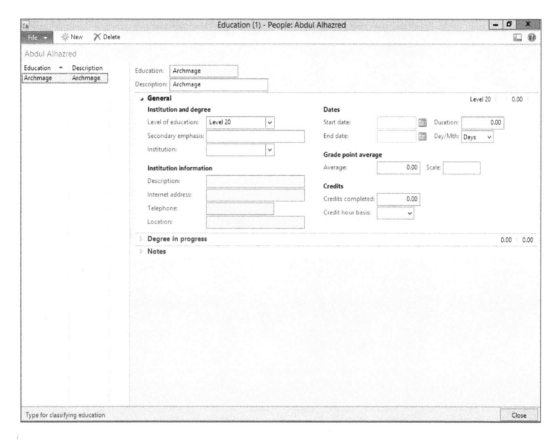

When the Education maintenance form is displayed, you can add any Education details you like against the Applicant.

Track Skills And Education Against Everyone To Help Match People To Jobs

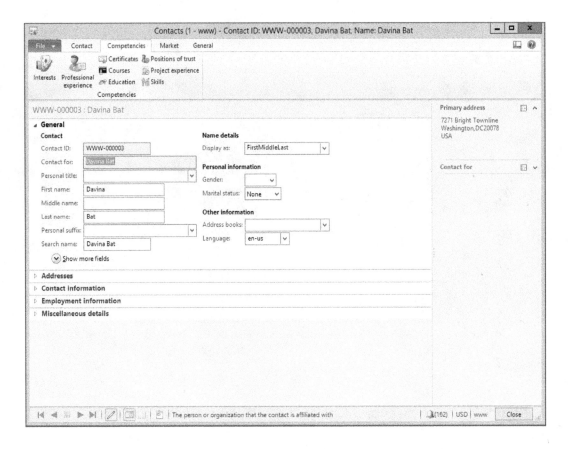

Finally, if you want to even track the Skills and Education against contacts (in essence every contact in Dynamics AX) then just open up the Contact record and click on the Education button within the Competencies group of the Competencies tab.

Track Skills And Education Against Everyone To Help Match People To Jobs

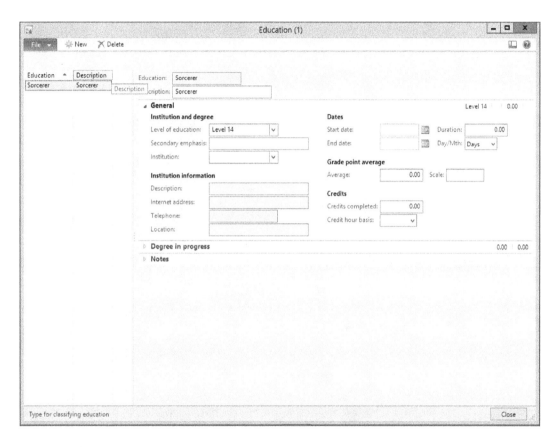

When the Education maintenance form is displayed, you can add any Education details you like against the Contact as well.

Track Skills And Education Against Everyone To Help Match People To Jobs

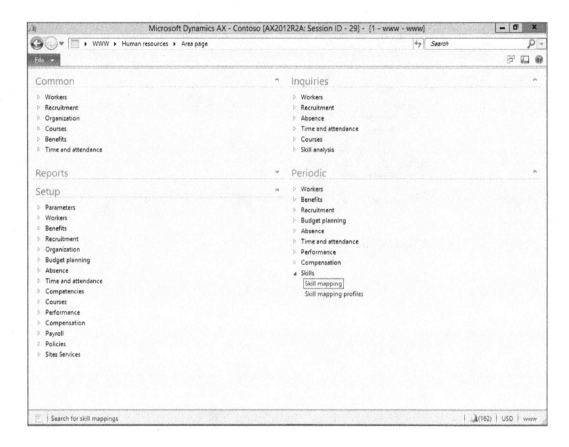

A quick way to search for people that have certain skills, click on the Skill Mapping menu item within the Skills folder of the Periodic group within the Human Resources area page.

Track Skills And Education Against Everyone To Help Match People To Jobs

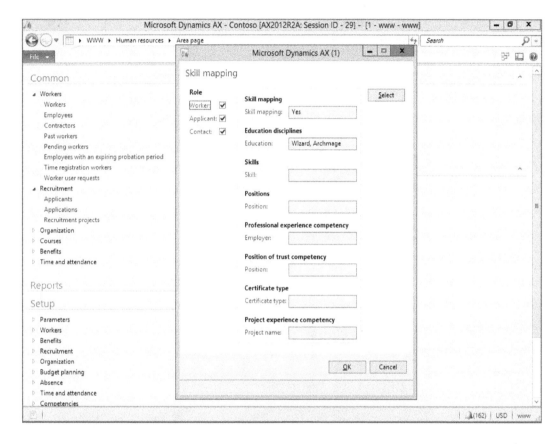

When the Skill Mapping dialog box is displayed, set the Selection criteria to match the Skills and Education that you need, and then click on the OK button.

Track Skills And Education Against Everyone To Help Match People To Jobs

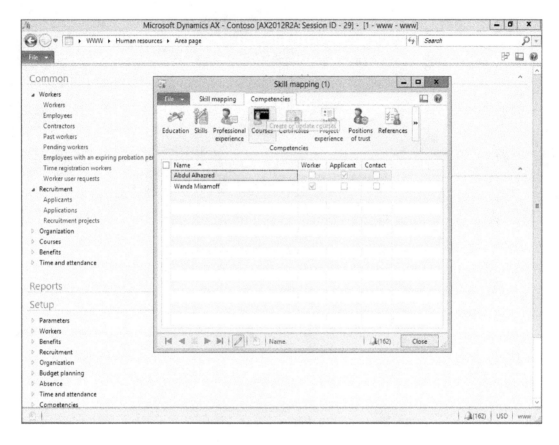

This will return a list of Workers, Contacts and Applicants that match your search.

How cool is that!

Add Media To Questionnaires To Create Visual Training Exercises And Certifications

Questionnaires are a great way within Dynamics AX to gather information, but you are not just limited to using text in them. There is an option that also allows you to associate media files with individual questions that are showed in conjunction with the questions.

This allows you to create visual training and testing Questionnaires that you can assign to employees to complete if you have training and certification requirements.

Add Media To Questionnaires To Create Visual Training Exercises And Certifications

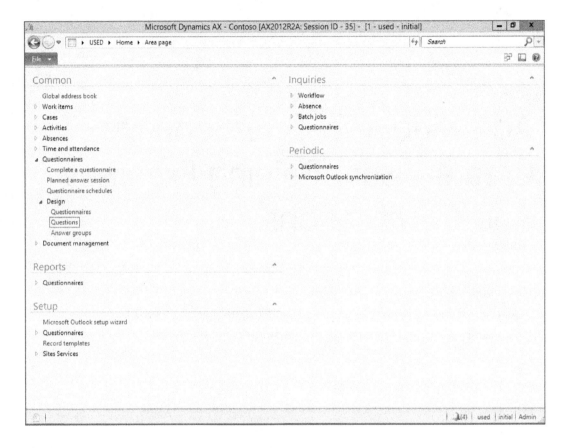

Select the Questions menu item from within the Design subfolder of the Questionnaires folder in the Common group of the Home area page.

Add Media To Questionnaires To Create Visual Training Exercises And Certifications

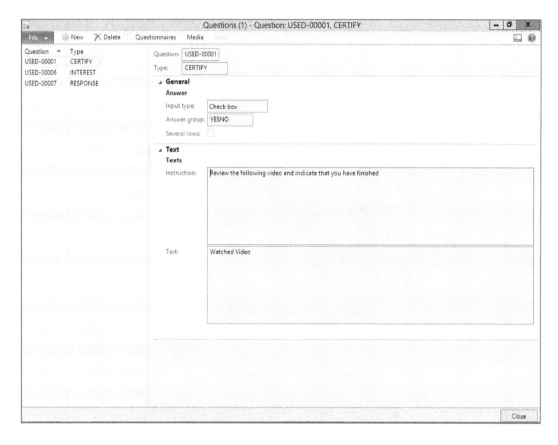

When the Questions maintenance form is displayed, click on the New button in the menu bar to create a new question.

Set the Input Type to Checkbox, and give your question some Instructions and also the Text prompt.

Then click on the Media button in the menu bar.

Add Media To Questionnaires To Create Visual Training Exercises And Certifications

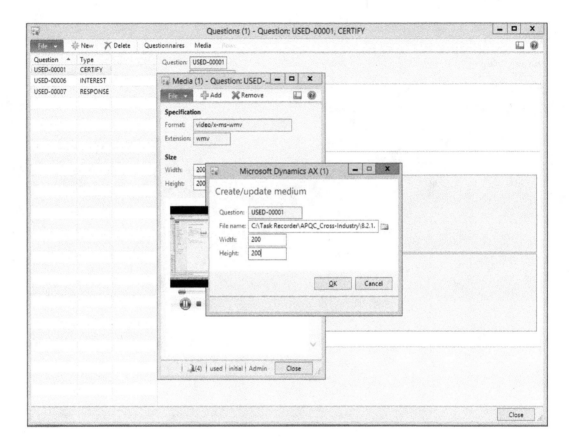

When the Media dialog box is displayed, click on the Add button in the menu bar to associate some media to the question.

When the Create/update medium dialog box is displayed, specify the Filename and also the Width and Height and then click on the OK button.

Add Media To Questionnaires To Create Visual Training Exercises And Certifications

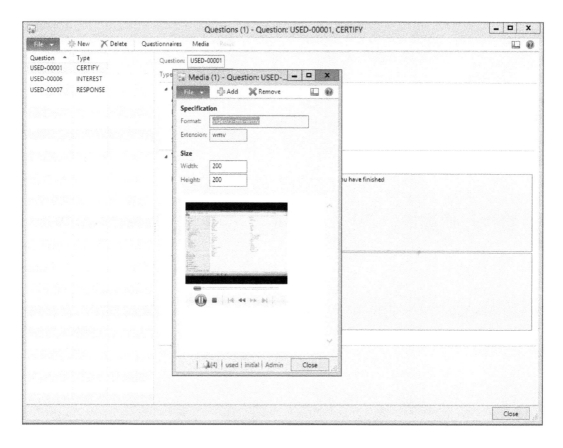

When you return to the Media dialog box you should be able to see the animation that you added.

Add Media To Questionnaires To Create Visual Training Exercises And Certifications

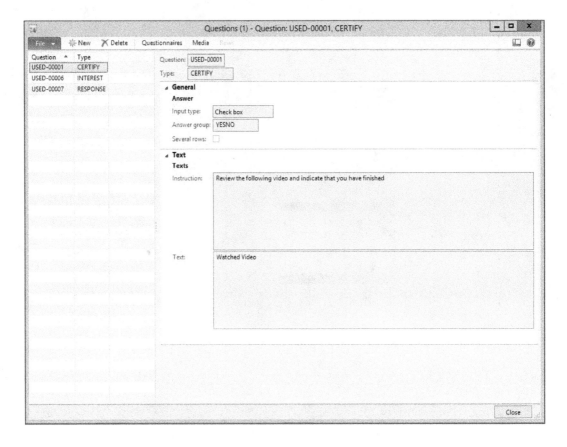

Repeat the addition of the Question, but this time, specify the question that you want associated with the video.

When you have finished, just click on the Close button to exit from the form.

Add Media To Questionnaires To Create Visual Training Exercises And Certifications

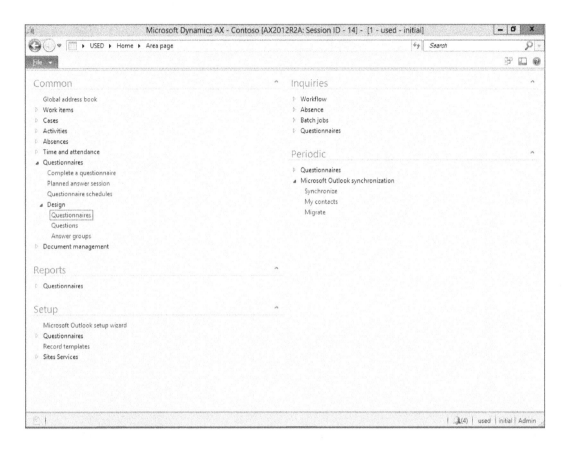

Next, select the Questionnaires menu item from within the Design subfolder of the Questionnaires folder in the Common group of the Home area page.

Add Media To Questionnaires To Create Visual Training Exercises And Certifications

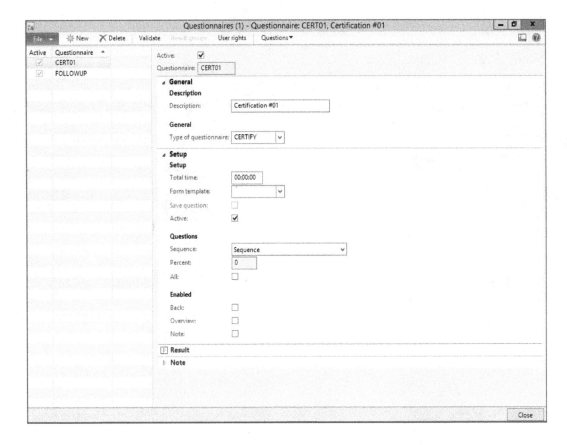

When the Questionnaires maintenance form is displayed, click on the New button in the menu bar to create a new questionnaire.

Assign your Questionnaire a name and a Description.

Add Media To Questionnaires To Create Visual Training Exercises And Certifications

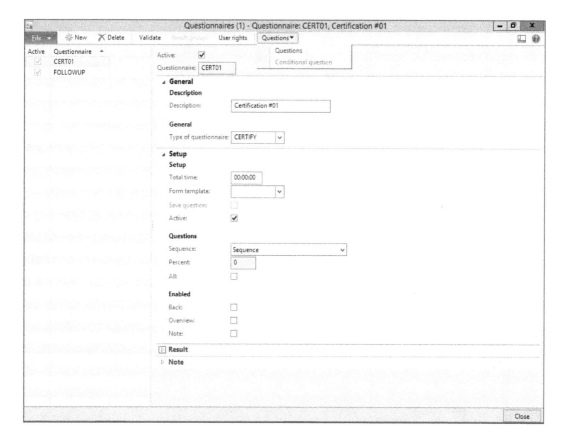

Now click on the Questions button on the menu bar, and select the Questions menu item.

Add Media To Questionnaires To Create Visual Training Exercises And Certifications

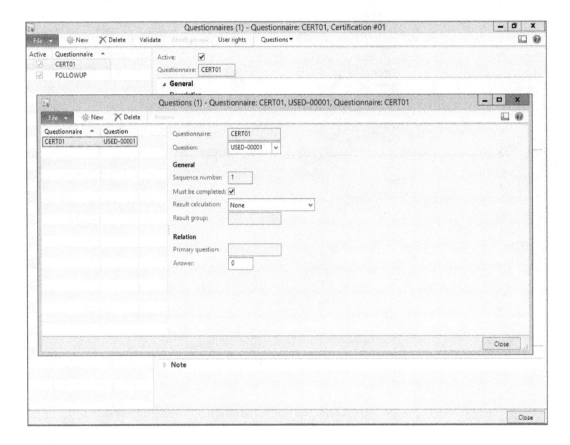

When the Questions maintenance form is displayed, click the New button in the menu bar to add a new question.

From the Question dropdown, select the first question that you just added.

Repeat the process again for the second question, and then click the close button to exit from the form, and return to the main menu.

Add Media To Questionnaires To Create Visual Training Exercises And Certifications

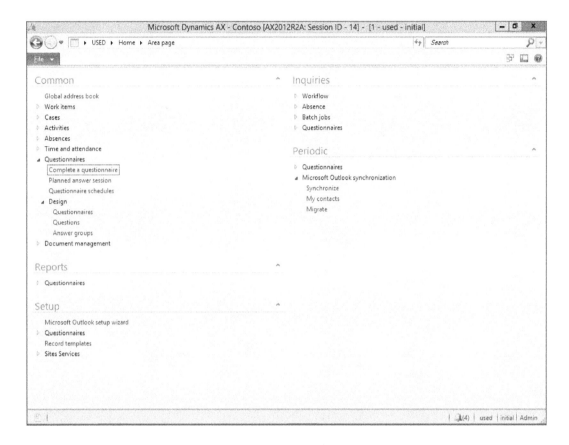

To test the Questionnaire, select the Complete a questionnaires menu item from within the Questionnaires folder in the Common group of the Home area page.

Add Media To Questionnaires To Create Visual Training Exercises And Certifications

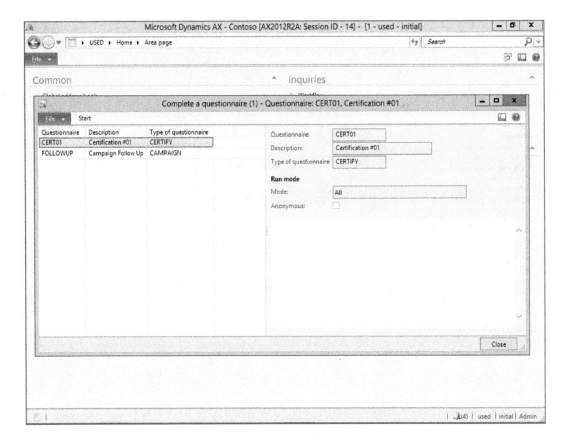

Select the Questionnaire and click the Start button in the menu bar.

Add Media To Questionnaires To Create Visual Training Exercises And Certifications

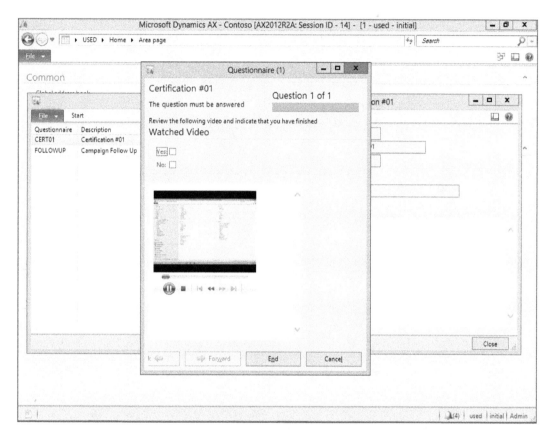

You will now see the first question, along with the animated media. After you have viewed it, just click on the Forward button to move to the next question.

Now you have to answer the test question, and you can click End when you are finished.

Drilling Into AX Detail Directly From The Management Reporter Web Viewer

If you use Management Reporter, then you probably already know that you can drill into the Dynamics AX transactions directly from the Windows based report viewer. You can also do the same through the web based viewer, which is so much cooler.

Now you can browse through your financial reports on your Surface knowing that you can always get back to your detail at any time.

Drilling Into AX Detail Directly From The Management Reporter Web Viewer

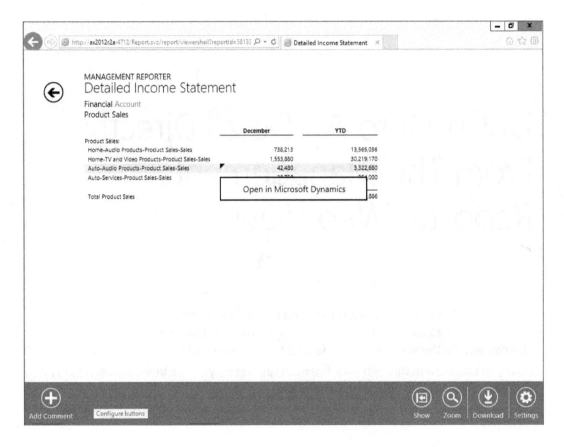

In the Management Reporter web client, select the line item that you want to drill into.

A small triangle will appear in the top left hand corner of the cell that will open up a link to Open in Microsoft Dynamics which you can click on.

Drilling Into AX Detail Directly From The Management Reporter Web Viewer

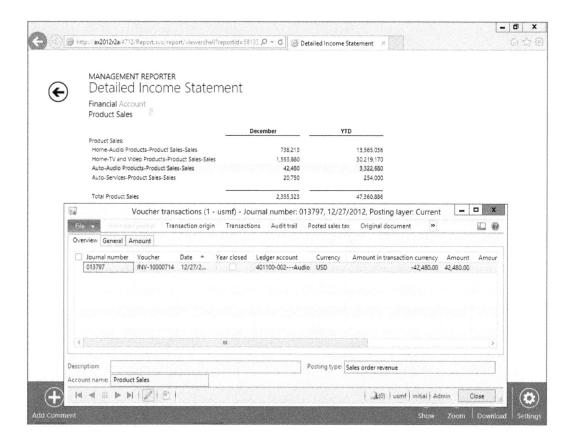

The Voucher Transactions form will the open within the Dynamics AX client allowing you to drill into the source data.

Use Excel Worksheets To Make Entering Budgeting A Breeze

At first glance, entering in all of your budgets within Dynamics AX may seem like a daunting prospect, because it looks like you need to break all of your budget entries out by account, and then by period. But it's not really the case. You can link all of your budget with Excel templates that you can then use to make the entry an extremely simple task.

Budgeting within Dynamics AX does not have to be a painful process.

Use Excel Worksheets To Make Entering Budgeting A Breeze

When you are assigned a budget to update, rather than entering in the budget line by line, and period by period, just click on the Worksheet button within the Supplemental group of the Budget Plan ribbon bar.

Use Excel Worksheets To Make Entering Budgeting A Breeze

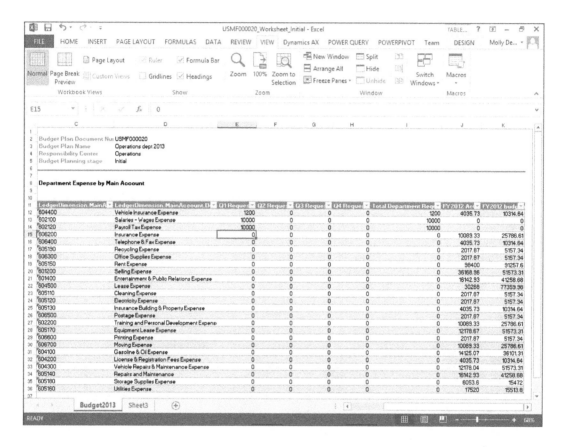

This will open up the budget entry template within Excel, and populate it with all of your budget detail.

Use Excel Worksheets To Make Entering Budgeting A Breeze

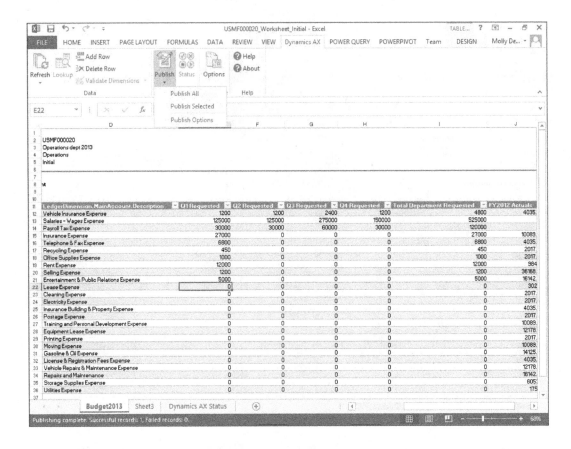

All you have to do now is update all of the budgets by account and period, and then click on the Publish All option of the Publish menu button within the Update group of the Dynamics AX ribbon bar.

Use Excel Worksheets To Make Entering Budgeting A Breeze

Now when you return to your budget detail within Dynamics AX, you will see that it has added records for you for all of the new budget entry records, and updated all of the budget figures with the values that you entered in the worksheet.

Also, you can always return to the worksheet by clicking on it within the Budget Plan Documents fact box.

How cool is that!

Assign Shortcut Keys To POS Terminal Buttons

Even through the Point Of Sale screens that are available for Dynamics AX are designed to be poked and prodded through touchscreens, if you are a keyboard jockey, then you may want to be able to use shortcut keys to get around to speed things up a little. If you don't have any shortcuts already defined, then you can easily do this directly within the POS application.

Now you will be able to zip around within the POS screens faster than Neo in The Matrix.

Assign Shortcut Keys To POS Terminal Buttons

To add a shortcut key to any button on the POS screen, just right-mouse-click on it and select the Button Properties option.

Assign Shortcut Keys To POS Terminal Buttons

When the Configure Button form is displayed, just change the Text on Button field to include a description that has an "&" before the letter that you want to use as the shortcut key.

When you are done then just click the OK button.

Assign Shortcut Keys To POS Terminal Buttons

In this example, I can start off on the main form of the POS Register, and then press ALT-V.

Assign Shortcut Keys To POS Terminal Buttons

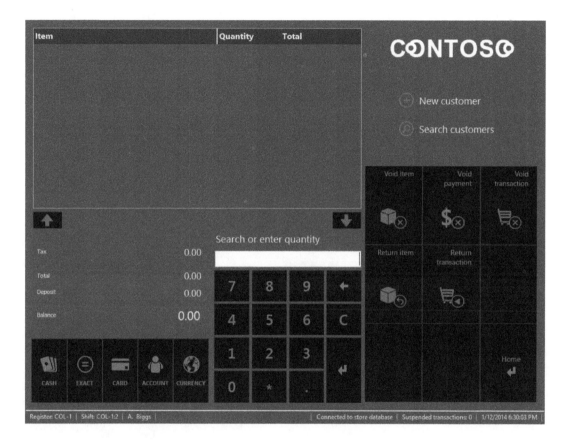

And I will be taken straight into the Voids and Returns sub-menu.

OFFICE TRICKS

It's no secret that everyone uses Office to create documents and reports, and that's fine. But if you really want to use Office, then you should take advantage of all the integration that is built into it for Dynamics AX.

Don't just cut and paste your spreadsheets, link them to Dynamics AX. Don't just use Excel as a worksheet to help you with your updates, make it the way that you update Dynamics AX. Don't just copy data to Word documents, make them templates that are automatically updated. Don't just use Project for recording project information, make it a tool that updates Dynamics AX.

In this section we will uncover how you can use some of the integrated Office features to make you a Dynamics AX ninja.

Make the Dynamics AX Role Center Your Outlook Home Page

The Role Centers are web pages that you can run independently of the client, and are designed to give you a lightweight way to access most of the functions within Dynamics AX. Since they are just web pages then they can also be embedded in other applications that you may use all of the time, like Outlook, to give you another way to view the status of the organization.

This is a great way to let users that are not normally accessing Dynamics AX all of the time view the status of the organization, since they cannot avoid opening up Outlook.

Make the Dynamics AX Role Center Your Outlook Home Page

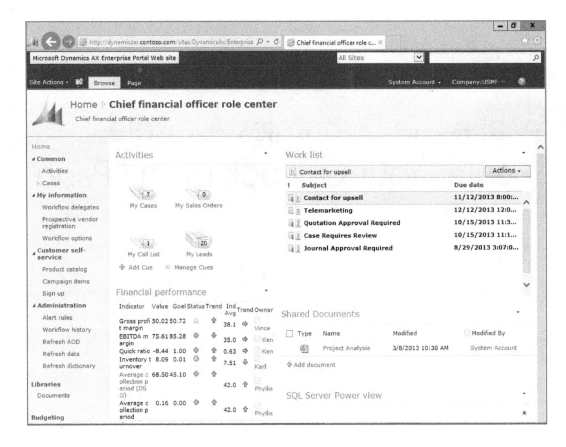

Access the Enterprise Portal through a web browser. The usual website address is:

http://servername/sites/DynamicsAx/Enterprise%20Portal/

Note: When you open up the Enterprise Portal through the browser, you will get a little more information that you do when it is seen within the Dynamics AX client. You have a title bar along the top, and also a web menu bar on the left.

Make the Dynamics AX Role Center Your Outlook Home Page

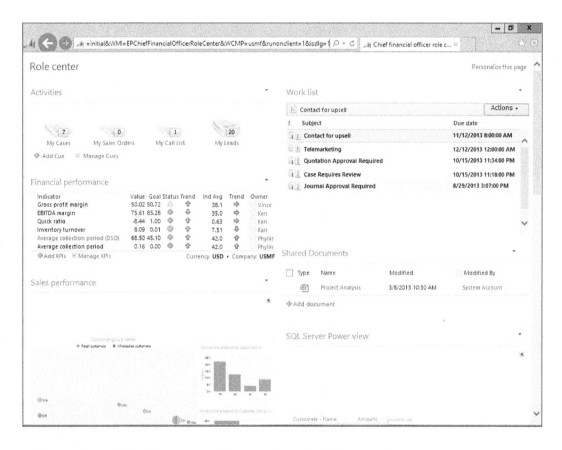

If you add the following two qualifiers to the end of the URL, then your Enterprise Portal will become a lot cleaner.

&runonclient=1&isdlg=1

Make the Dynamics AX Role Center Your Outlook Home Page

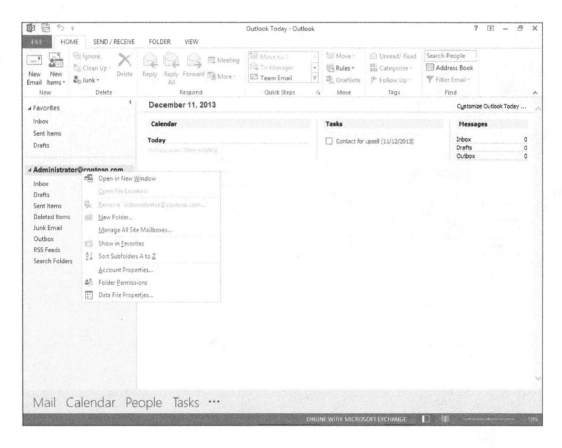

Now open up Outlook, and right-mouse-click on your account header and select the Data File Properties menu item.

Make the Dynamics AX Role Center Your Outlook Home Page

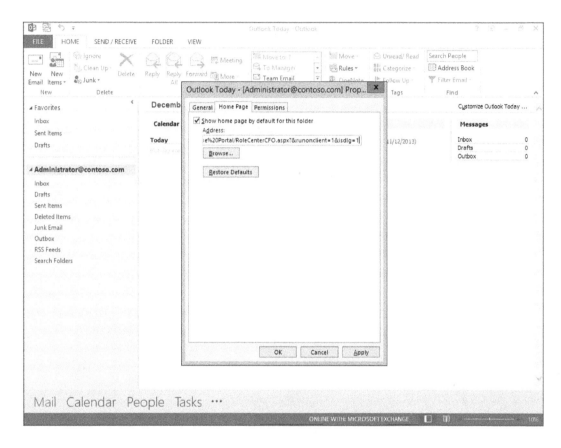

When the Data File Properties dialog box is displayed, click on the Home Page tab, and past the role center URL into the Address field. The format will look something like this:

http://servername/sites/DynamicsAx/Enterprise%20Portal/RoleCenterCFO.aspx?&run onclient=1&isdlg=1

Make the Dynamics AX Role Center Your Outlook Home Page

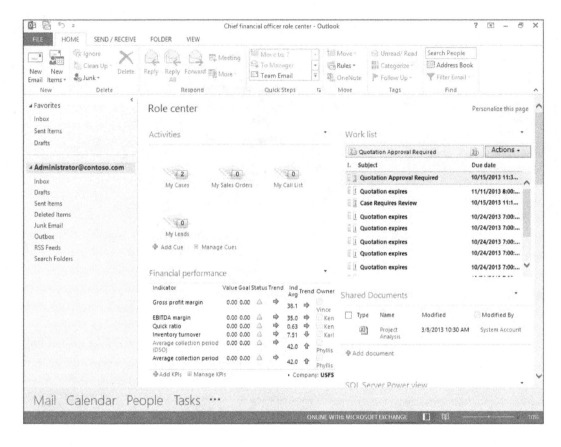

Now when you return to Outlook, you will see the Role Center as the Outlook home page.

Use Lync to Track People Down Directly From Dynamics AX

Lync is a great way to communicate with all of the people that you work with since you can easily see if people are available, and then instantly start an instant message, voice call, or a video conferencing session. It is also fully integrated with Dynamics AX, allowing you to start Lync communications without even having to search for the person within Lync.

This is a great tool for the users because they can instantly connect with other people in the company, especially when you are researching a problem, or want to ask questions about something that was entered into Dynamics AX by someone else. All you have to do is click and call.

Use Lync to Track People Down Directly From Dynamics AX

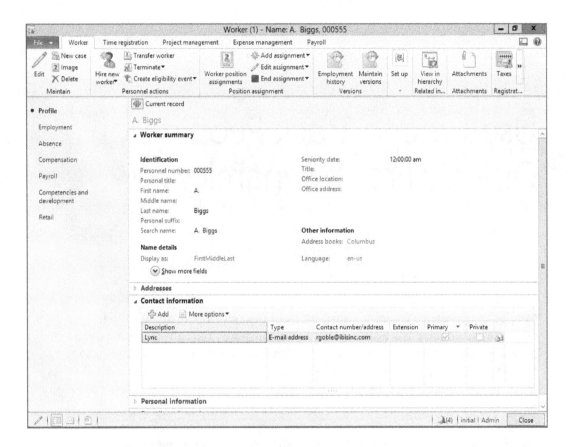

There is one setup step that is required in order to enable to Lync with the people within the organization, and that is to tell Dynamics AX what email address to use for the people when searching for them through Lync.

To do this you need to open up the Worker records, and make sure that their Lync email address is registered against the Contact Information.

Use Lync to Track People Down Directly From Dynamics AX

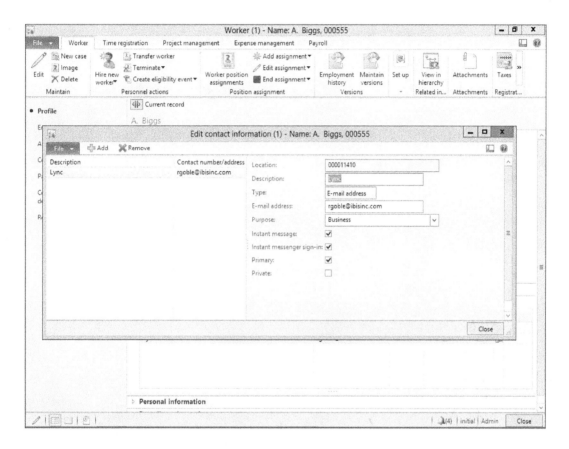

You also need to check that the Instant message and Instant message sign-in flags are checked against the Lync email address.

Use Lync to Track People Down Directly From Dynamics AX

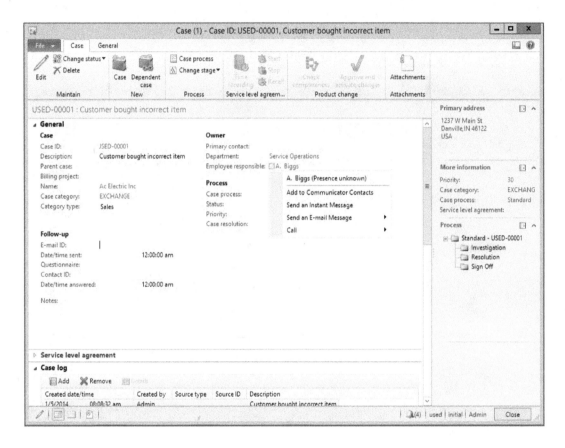

Now when you see any of the users referenced within Dynamics AX, you will see the Lync presence bubble, and if you click on the bubble, you will be able to start Lync calls directly from there.

Synchronize Dynamics AX With Microsoft Outlook

Although we would like to be sitting in front of Dynamics AX all the time, it's usually just not the case because we're travelling, or just away from our desks. All that time, people may be setting up meetings for you, assigning critical tasks, or updating contact information that maybe you will need.

You don't have to miss a beat though because you can set up your Dynamics AX client so that it synchronizes with Microsoft Outlook, and then all of the tasks, appointments, and contacts that you use will travel with you on your laptop, tablet, and even your phone.

Synchronize Dynamics AX With Microsoft Outlook

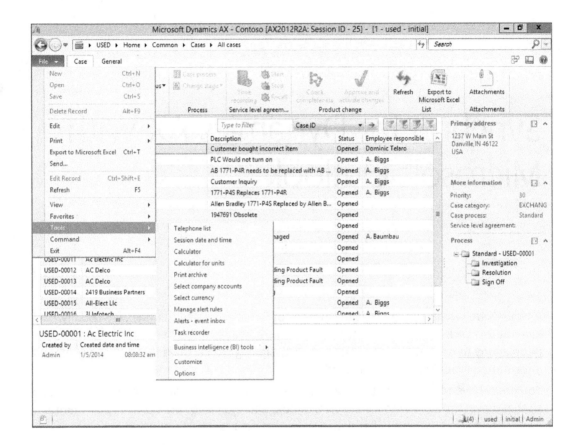

Before we start, there is one small piece of housekeeping that you need to perform before configuring the synchronization. Dynamics AX and Outlook pair themselves through the e-mail account that is associated with your client. So start off by selecting the Options menu item from the Tools submenu of the Files menu.

Synchronize Dynamics AX With Microsoft Outlook

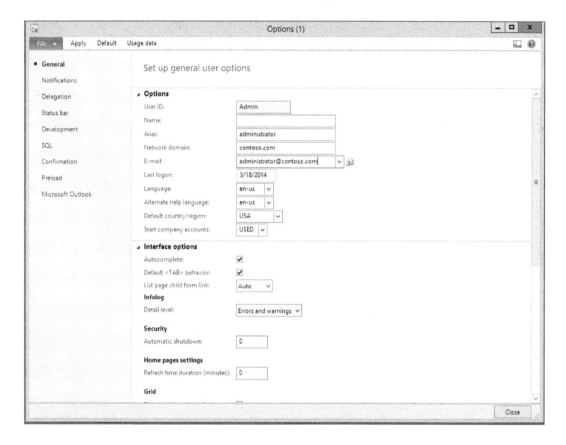

When the Options dialog box is displayed, check that the E-mail account is the same as the account that you use for Microsoft Outlook.

Synchronize Dynamics AX With Microsoft Outlook

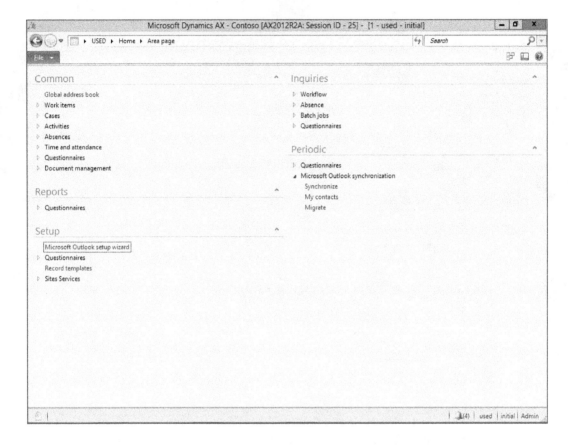

To set up the pairing between your Dynamics AX client and Outlook, select the Microsoft Outlook setup wizard option from the Setup group of the Home area page.

Synchronize Dynamics AX With Microsoft Outlook

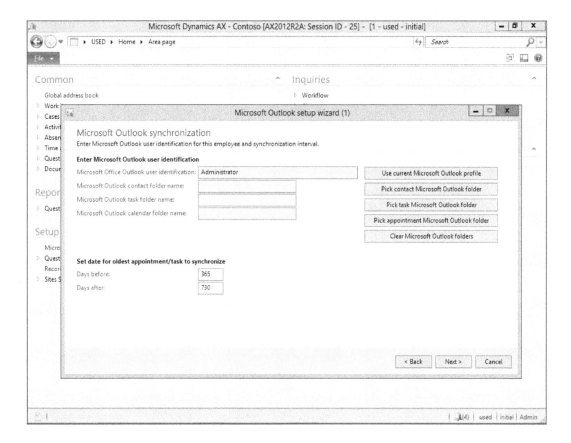

Step through the wizard until you get to the Microsoft Outlook synchronization page, and click on the Use current Microsoft Outlook profile button to link the profiles. If your e-mail addresses match then your name should show up in the Microsoft Office Outlook user identification field.

Synchronize Dynamics AX With Microsoft Outlook

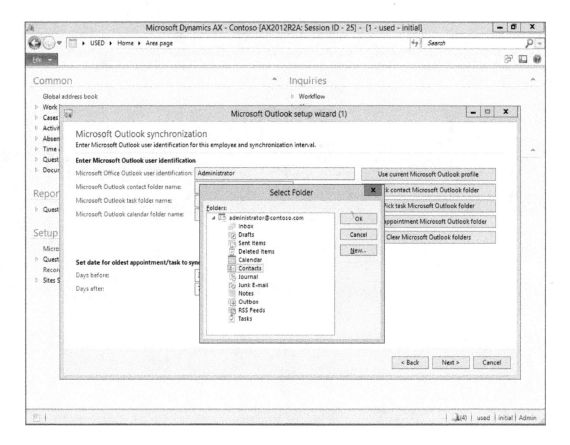

Next click on the Pick contact Microsoft Outlook folder button, and choose the folder in Outlook that you want to synchronize the contacts to.

Synchronize Dynamics AX With Microsoft Outlook

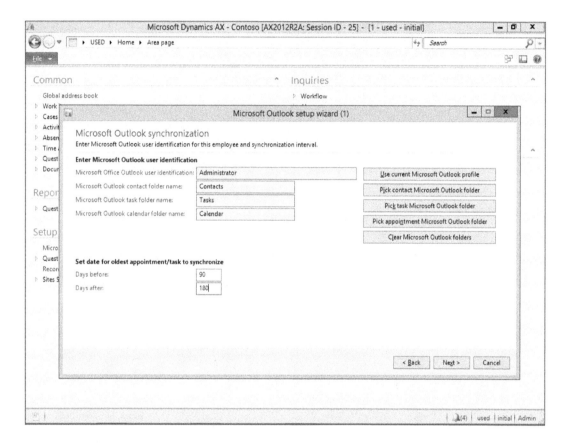

Repeat this for the tasks, and also the appointments, and then set a number of days in the past and future that you want to synchronize.

Then you can continue through the wizard and exit the setup.

Synchronize Dynamics AX With Microsoft Outlook

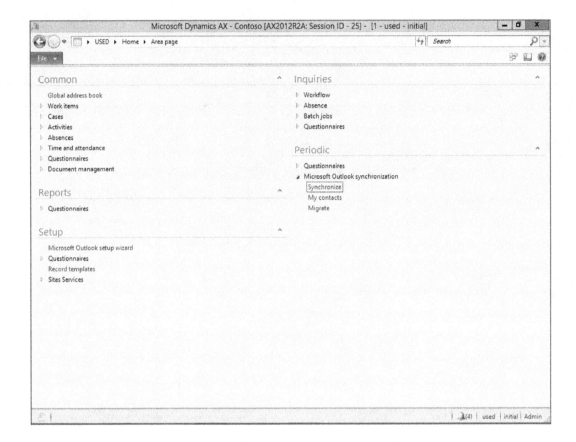

To synchronize Dynamics AX with Outlook, just click on the Synchronize menu item within the Microsoft Outlook synchronization folder of the Periodic group of the Home area page.

Synchronize Dynamics AX With Microsoft Outlook

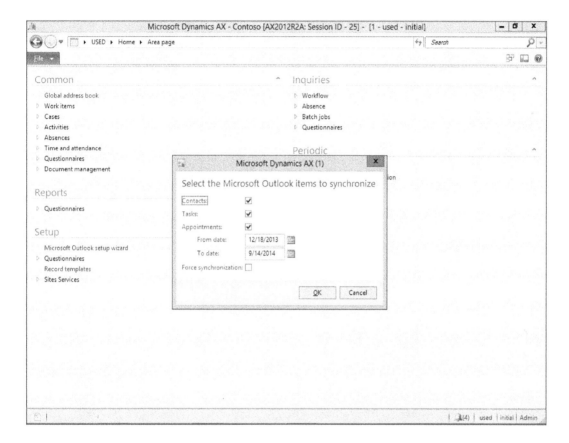

Select the elements that you want to synchronize, and then click the OK button to synchronize.

Synchronize Dynamics AX With Microsoft Outlook

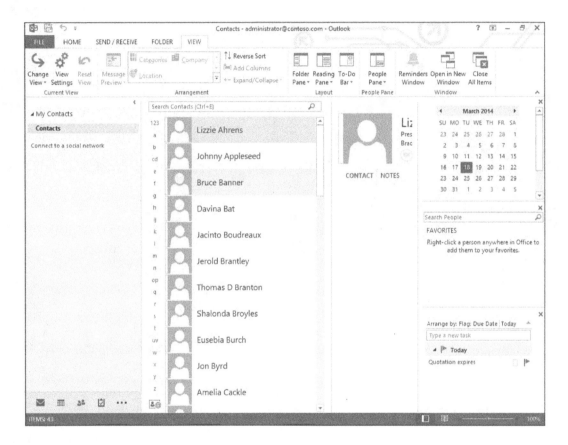

Now all of your appointments, tasks, and contacts will be over in Outlook.

Synchronize Your Contacts Between Dynamics AX And Outlook And Back Again

If you have linked Dynamics AX with your local version of Microsoft Outlook, then you have probably ran the synchronization that adds all of the appointments, tasks, and also the contacts to Outlook. But there is a more powerful option that allows you to synchronize not only from Dynamics AX and Outlook, but with Outlook back to Dynamics AX giving you an even more useful form of contact synchronization.

This is a great way to keep your contacts up to date, and also to populate Dynamics AX with all of your contact data without having to key in all of the people by hand, and also keep it up to date because it synchronizes both ways.

Remember, a contact does not become less useful if you share it with your friends.

Synchronize Your Contacts Between Dynamics AX And Outlook And Back Again

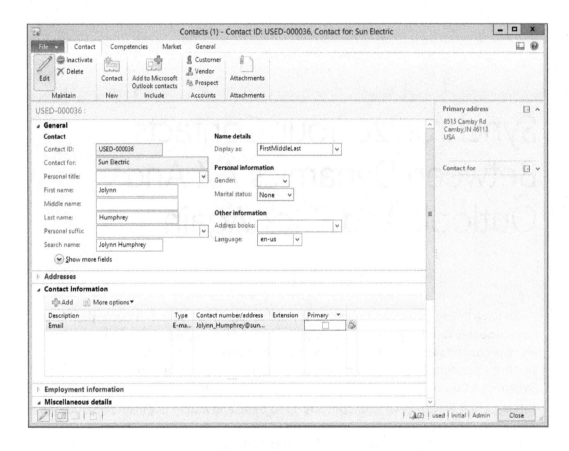

Start of by adding contacts to Dynamics AX.

Synchronize Your Contacts Between Dynamics AX And Outlook And Back Again

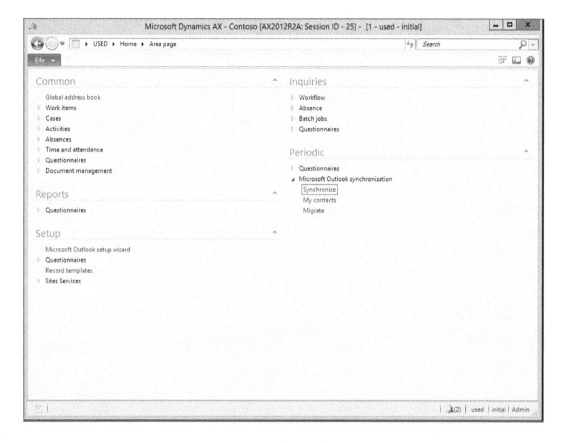

Then click on the Synchronize menu item within the Microsoft Outlook Synchronization folder of the Periodic group of the Home area page.

Synchronize Your Contacts Between Dynamics AX And Outlook And Back Again

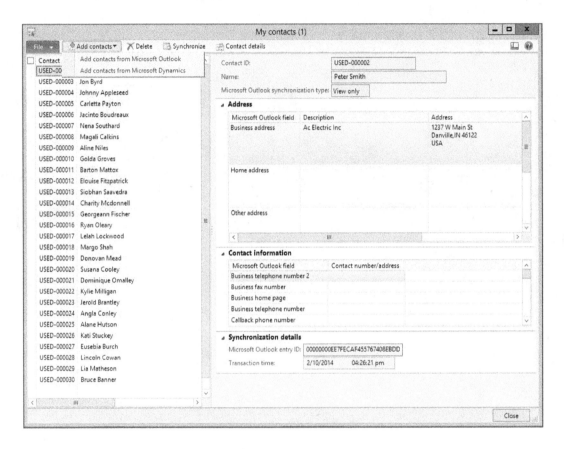

When the My Contacts maintenance form is displayed, to synchronize the contacts within Dynamics AX to Outlook, click on the Add contacts from Microsoft Dynamics menu item under the Add contacts menu item.

Synchronize Your Contacts Between Dynamics AX And Outlook And Back Again

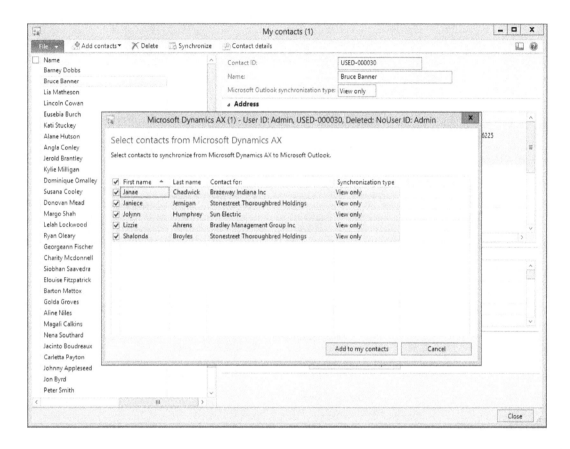

When the Select contacts from Microsoft Dynamics AX dialog box is displayed, all of the contacts that have not currently been synchronized with Outlook will be displayed. Check all of the contacts that you want to synchronize and then click on the Add to my contacts button.

Synchronize Your Contacts Between Dynamics AX And Outlook And Back Again

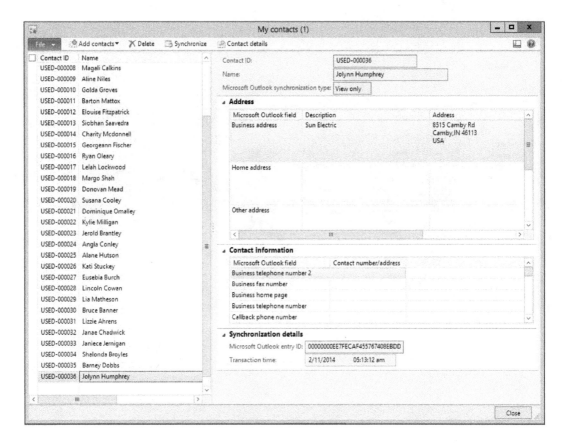

When you return to My contacts all the contacts will now have an link back to Outlook.

Synchronize Your Contacts Between Dynamics AX And Outlook And Back Again

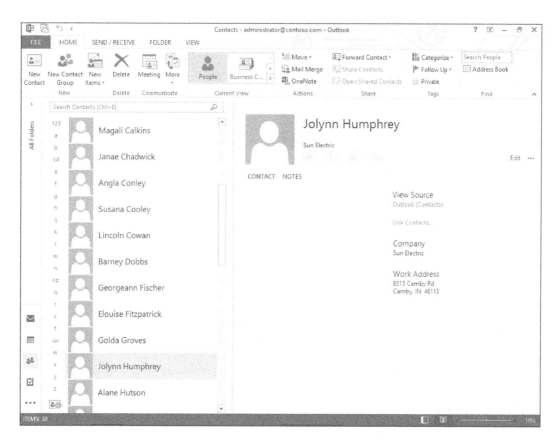

If you open up Outlook then all of the contact information will be synchronized.

Synchronize Your Contacts Between Dynamics AX And Outlook And Back Again

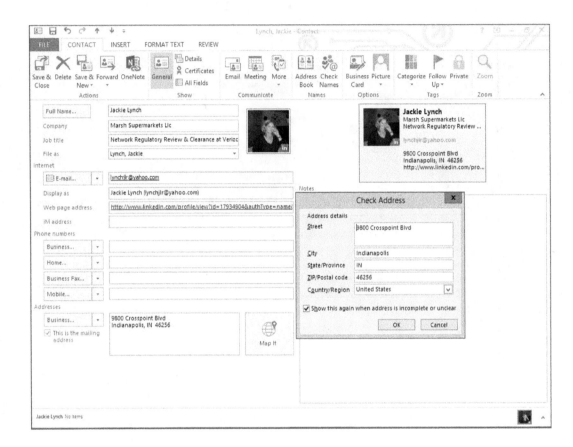

Next, add a contact within Outlook that doesn't exist within Dynamics AX.

One tip is to ensure that the Country/Region for the address is United States.

Synchronize Your Contacts Between Dynamics AX And Outlook And Back Again

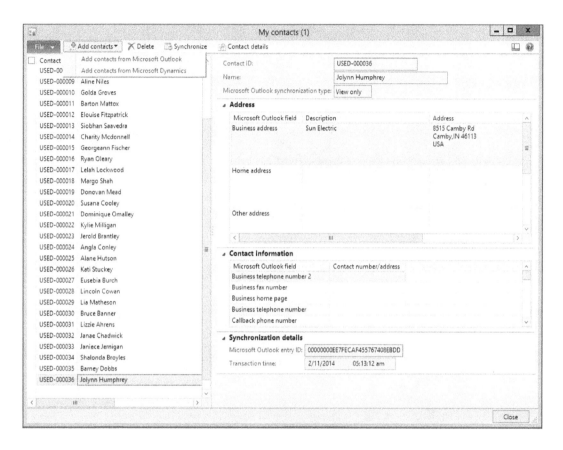

Return to the My Contacts maintenance form is displayed, and to synchronize the contacts within Outlook with Dynamics AX, click on the Add contacts from Microsoft Outlook menu item under the Add contacts menu item.

Synchronize Your Contacts Between Dynamics AX And Outlook And Back Again

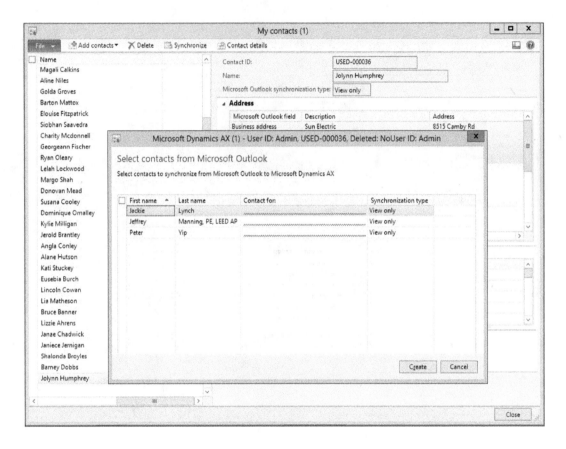

When the Select contacts from Microsoft Outlook dialog box is displayed, all of the contacts that have not currently been synchronized Outlook to Dynamics AX will be displayed.

Synchronize Your Contacts Between Dynamics AX And Outlook And Back Again

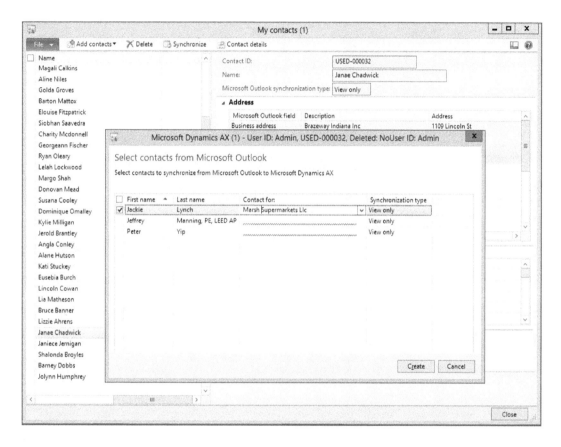

Check all of the contacts that you want to synchronize and also add the Contact for which will be the company that you want to associate the contact with.

When you are finished, click on the Create button.

Synchronize Your Contacts Between Dynamics AX And Outlook And Back Again

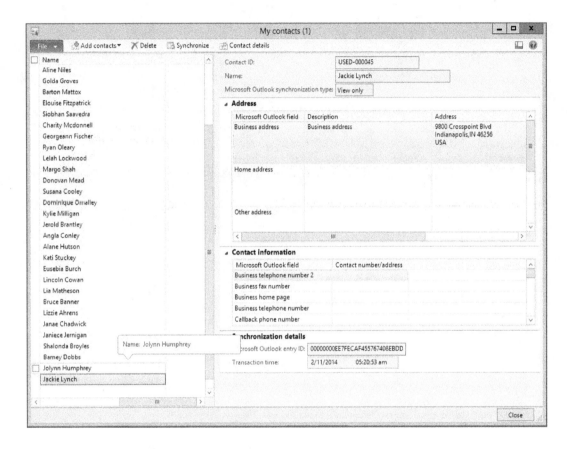

When you return to My contacts all the contacts from Outlook will now be added to the list of synchronized contacts.

Synchronize Your Contacts Between Dynamics AX And Outlook And Back Again

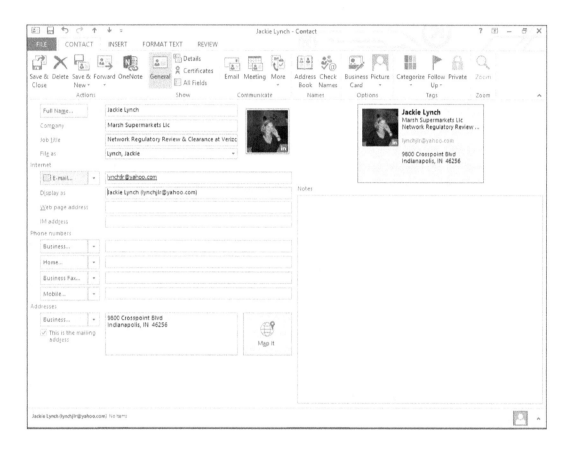

For any of the contacts, where they originated within Outlook, you can update the records information – like the phone number, or the email address.

Synchronize Your Contacts Between Dynamics AX And Outlook And Back Again

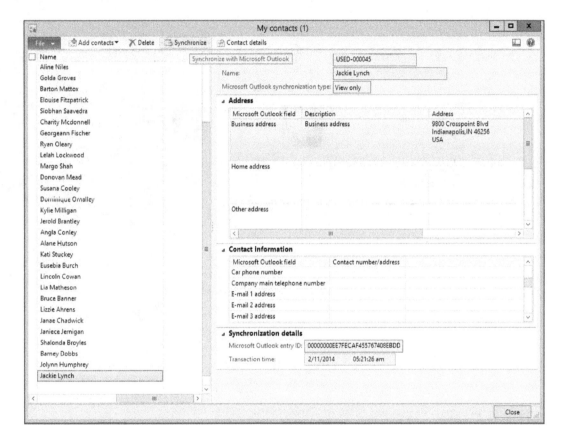

To update Dynamics AX, all you need to do is click on the Synchronize button within the menu bar of the My Contacts maintenance form.

Synchronize Your Contacts Between Dynamics AX And Outlook And Back Again

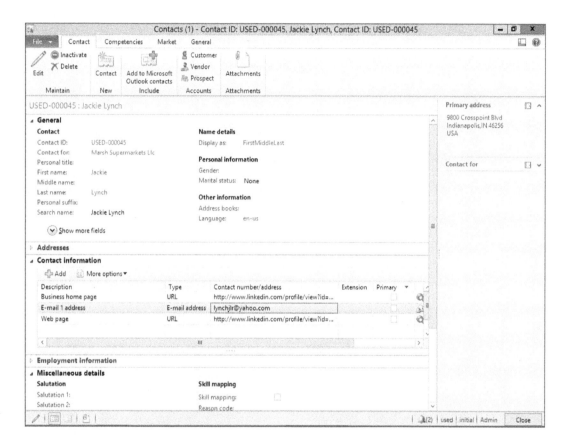

When you look at the contact within Dynamics AX, the details will be changed.

How slick is that!

REPORTING TIPS

Although the standard reports that are delivered with Dynamics AX are good, you can take your own reports up to the next level by taking advantage of some of the not to visible reporting tools that are available. You can take advantage of the cubes that are delivered with Dynamics AX, you can create dashboards using Excel and PowerView, and you can even publish out data directly from Dynamics AX to Office 365 so that you all can share queries and reports.

In this section we will show some of the ways that you can create and share reports that you may not be familiar with.

Create Reports Instantly With Autoreports

Sometimes you need to send someone a copy of all the data that you have on your current screen for reference. Although you can send them a screen shot, there is a much better option for you which is called an Autoreport. To create it, all you have to do is press CTRL-P and Dynamics AX will do the rest for you.

Autoreports are great because they will create reports on all of the data that you have in the query regardless of if you have multiple pages, they have hyperlinks back to the main data such as products making drilling into the information easier, and they are more secure since they can be delivered as PDF documents.

Forget the ALT-PRINTSCREEN key combination, and just remember CTRL-P.

Create Reports Instantly With Autoreports

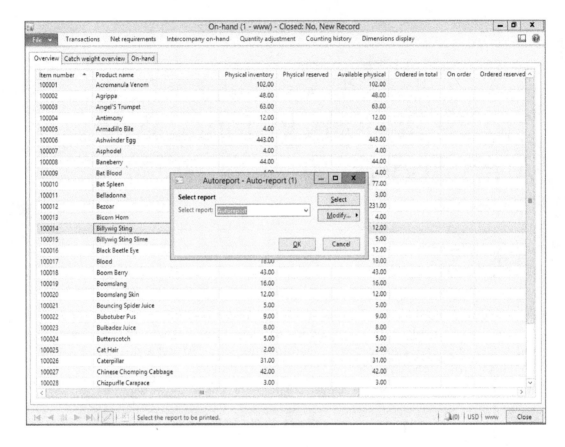

From the form that you want to export out as a report, just press CTRL-P. When the Autoreport dialog box shows up click the OK button to create the report.

Create Reports Instantly With Autoreports

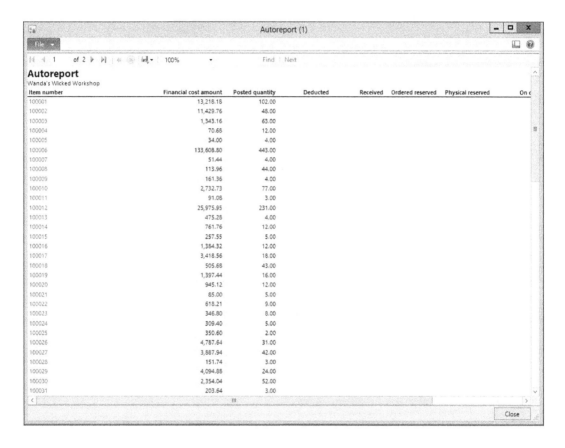

This will create a report for you showing exactly the same information that you had on-screen, filtered out to match the same data that you had queried.

Export To Excel When There Is No Ribbon Bar

Not all of the forms within Dynamics AX have the ribbon bar enabled with the Export to Excel icon handy for you to use when you want to gram a copy of the data, but that doesn't mean that there is no way to quickly get your data moved over to a linked worksheet.

All you need to do is select the Export to Microsoft Excel menu item from the Files menu, or for those of you that love shortcut keys, just press CTRL+T and Dynamics AX will create an Excel Workbook with all of the data from the form populated in it.

Export To Excel When There Is No Ribbon Bar

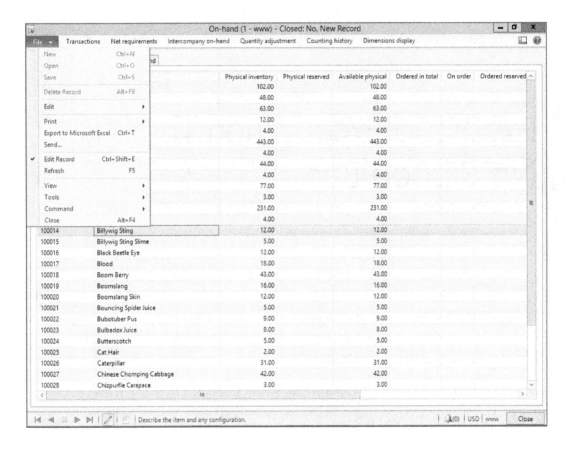

Select the Export to Microsoft Excel menu item from the Files menu.

Note: Your can also just press CTRL+T if you like using keyboard shortcuts.

Export To Excel When There Is No Ribbon Bar

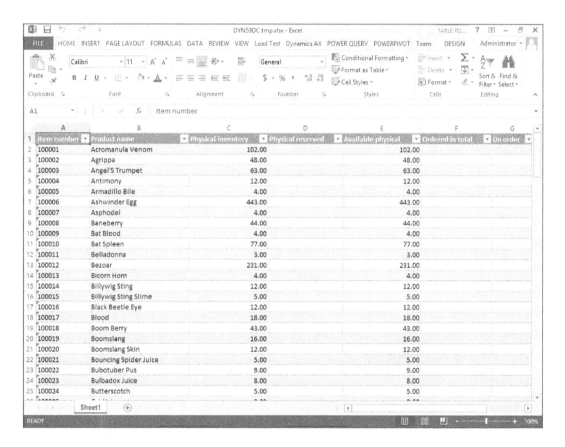

Now all of the data in the current form will be exported to a new Excel workbook.

Perform What-If Analysis Within Excel using PowerBI

Sometimes you want to have a way to juggle numbers a little to perform quick what-if analysis, but you are not committed to the change at the time so you really don't want to be changing the codes within Dynamics AX just yet, and would rather have the changes remain off-line until some time in the future.

In this example we will show you how to use an off-line worksheet that contains all of the changes that you want to make along with PowerPivot and PowerView to create a simple dashboard to track the impact that changes would have on your data.

Perform What-If Analysis Within Excel using PowerBI

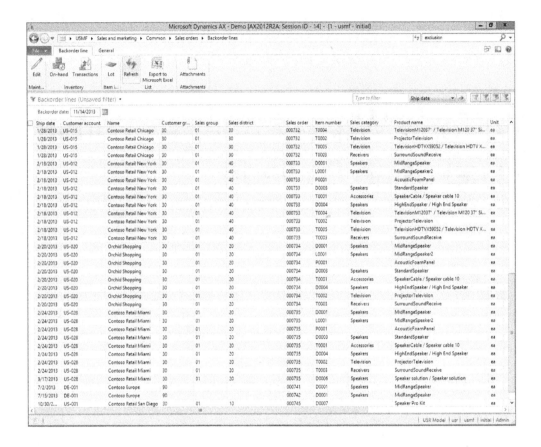

Before we start we will need some data to analyze. For this example we will get the backordered sales information. We made one small personalization change to the default form, and that was to add in the Customer Group, Sales Group, and Sales District for analysis.

We then just exported this information to Excel.

Perform What-If Analysis Within Excel using PowerBI

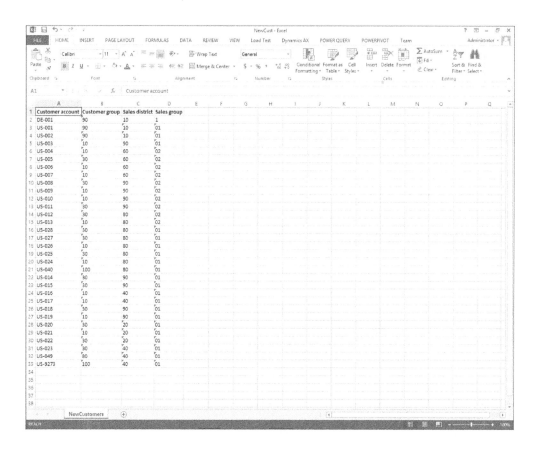

We will also need a worksheet that stores all of our alternate codings that we want to use for our What-If scenarios. Here we created a table that lists out all of the customers and their proposed groupings.

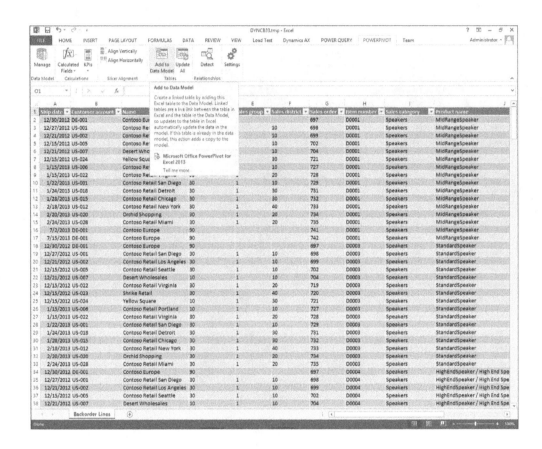

Once we have our Excel workbook with the linked data that we want to analyze, we will add it to a PowerPivot model by clicking on the Add to Data Model button within the Tables group of the POWERPIVOT ribbon bar.

Perform What-If Analysis Within Excel using PowerBI

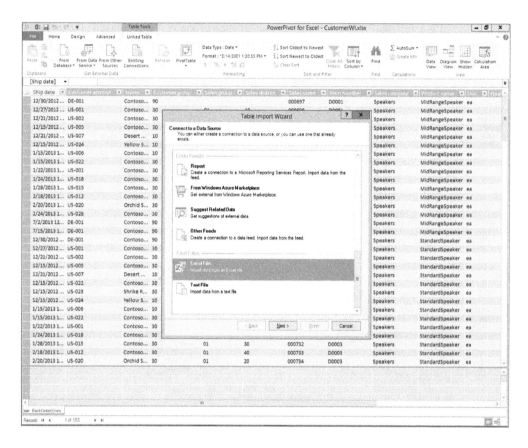

When the PowerPivot Manager window is displayed, click on the From Other Sources button within the Get External Data group of the Home ribbon bar, and select the Excel File option so that we can link in our What-If mappings.

Perform What-If Analysis Within Excel using PowerBI

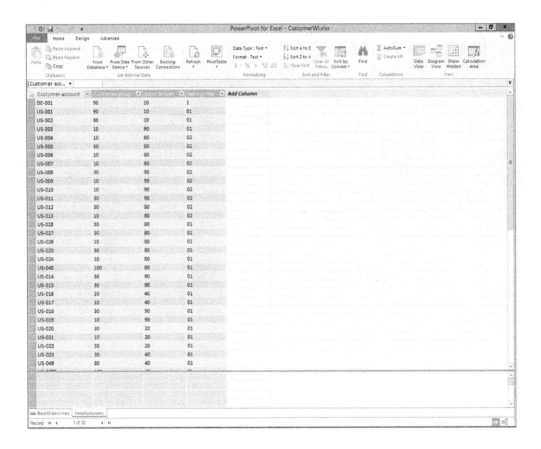

After choosing the worksheet that we created with the mew mappings, the data from the worksheet will be linked in with the PowerPivot model.

Perform What-If Analysis Within Excel using PowerBI

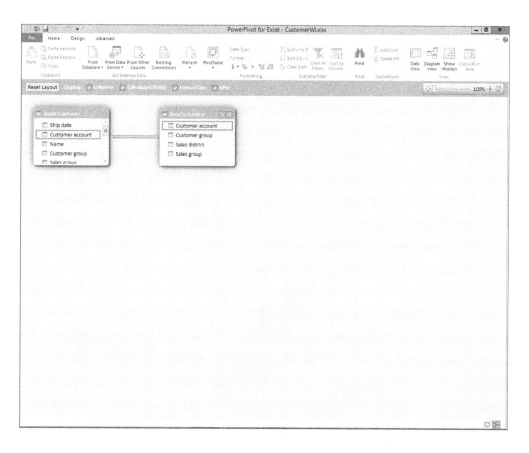

There is one last step that we need to perform here, and that is to link the tables. To do this, click on the Diagram View option within the View group of the Home ribbon bar and when the two tables are displayed, link them based off the Customer account. Now you can close out of the PowerPivot Manager.

Perform What-If Analysis Within Excel using PowerBI

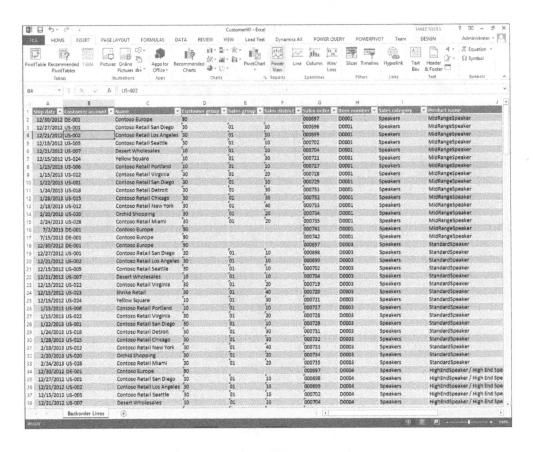

Now we can return to the Excel worksheet and create a new PowerView report based of the data by clicking on the PowerView menu item within the Reports group of the Insert ribbon bar.

Perform What-If Analysis Within Excel using PowerBI

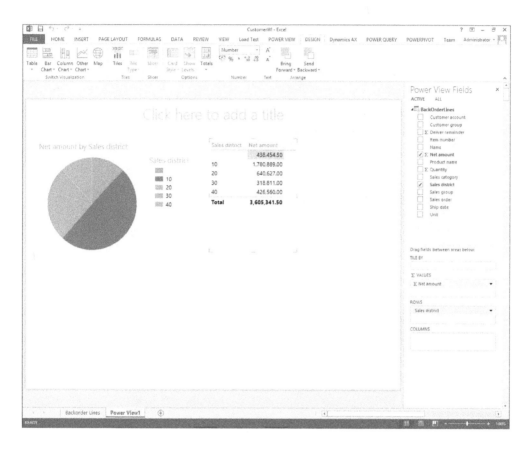

When the reporting canvas is displayed, you will be able to create a simple analysis based on the main (real) table data within the worksheet.

Perform What-If Analysis Within Excel using PowerBI

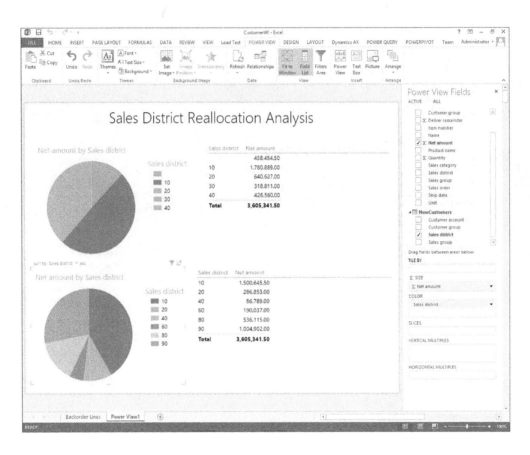

And you can create a second set of dashboard elements showing the data, but using the classifications that you have defined in the off-line worksheet.

Perform What-If Analysis Within Excel using PowerBI

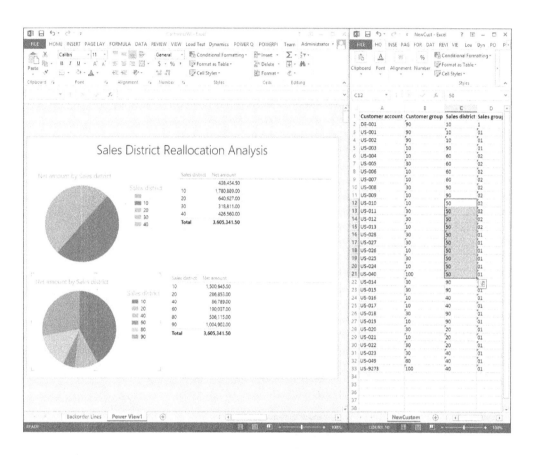

The great thing about this is that you can change the What-If classifications within the off-line worksheet...

Perform What-If Analysis Within Excel using PowerBI

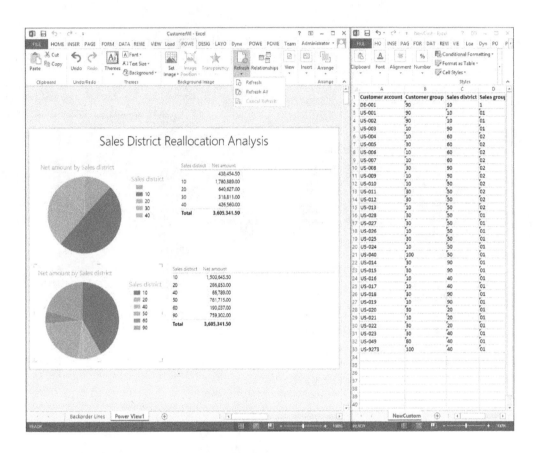

And if you click the Refresh button within the PowerView ribbon bar, the data will instantly change in the PowerView dashboard.

WORKFLOW TRICKS

Workflow is one of the most misunderstood areas of Dynamics AX, mainly because people think that it's complicated, and requires a developer to set it up and make it work properly. That is far from the case. A lot of the things that you can do with Workflow don't require you to write a single line of come, but add so much accountability to the users and the processes in the system.

In this section we will show some of the ways that you can use the Workflows to streamline your business processes.

Set Up A Workflow Delegate When You Are Not Available

Workflow is a great way to assign tasks to people and then track the progress of the tasks, because they are always visible, and never get misplaced or lost like the manual processes tend to allow. But sometimes you just have to take a break, and rather than having your workflow tasks languish until you get back, or even worse, follow you on vacation, use the delegation feature within Dynamics AX to route them to someone else that you trust.

Now you can sleep at night knowing that someone else is doing your work.

Set Up A Workflow Delegate When You Are Not Available

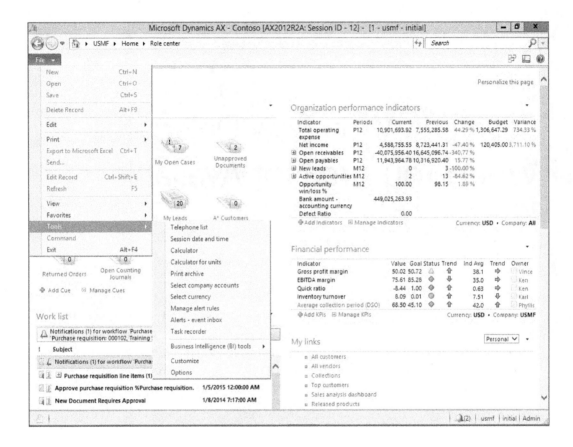

From the File menu, select the Tools submenu, and then click on the Options menu item.

Set Up A Workflow Delegate When You Are Not Available

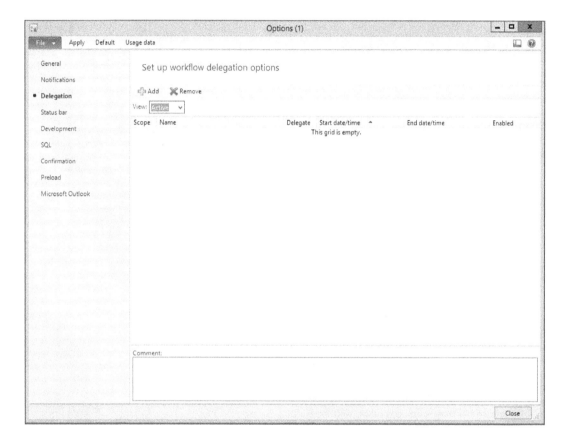

When the Options dialog box is displayed, change the tab group to Delegation, and then click on the Add button within the menu bar.

Set Up A Workflow Delegate When You Are Not Available

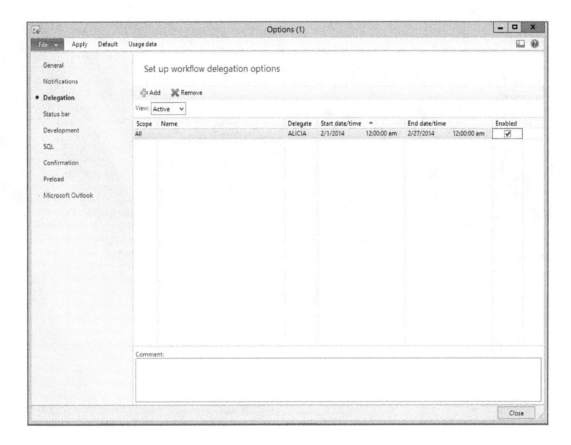

Now just say who you want to delegate all of your workflows to, set a from and to date, and then set it to be Enabled.

Dynamics AX will now route all of the workflows to your delegate.

Use Workflow Escalation To Make Sure Tasks Get Done

Workflows are great, because they allow you to control your business processes in a more efficient way than the traditional paper (or even worse word of mouth) and make sure that tasks don't get lost or forgotten. If you want to make them even more efficient then you can implement escalation rules that will assign tasks up the reporting chain when they are not done in a timely manner.

Like cream, workflow tasks can also float to the top...

Use Workflow Escalation To Make Sure Tasks Get Done

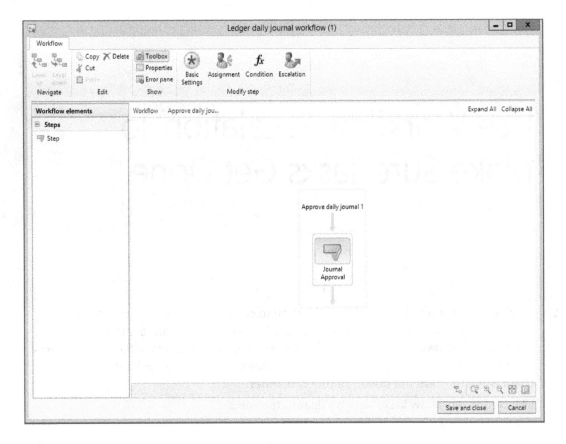

Open up your workflow design, and navigate to the element that you want to add the escalation rule to, and then then click on the Assignment button within the Modify Step group of the Workflow ribbon bar.

Use Workflow Escalation To Make Sure Tasks Get Done

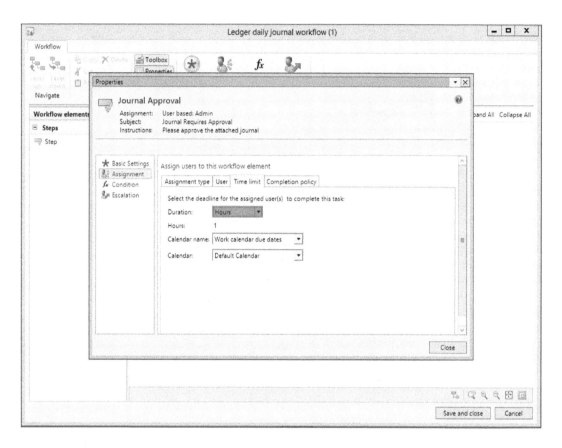

When the workflow step properties dialog box is displayed, select the Time Limit tab from the Assignment group, and set the expected time that you want the task to be performed within.

Use Workflow Escalation To Make Sure Tasks Get Done

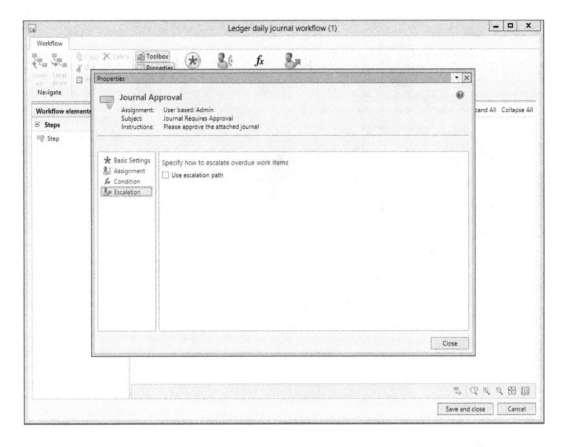

Now switch to the Escalation group, and check the Use Escalation Path checkbox to enable escalations.

Use Workflow Escalation To Make Sure Tasks Get Done

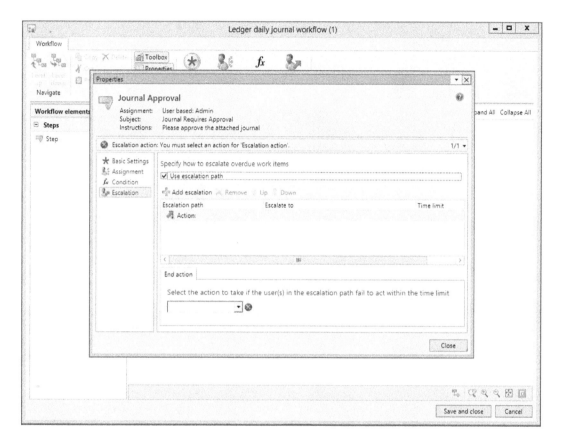

The Escalation tab will now expand to show you a number of new options that are used to define your Escalation Path.

Use Workflow Escalation To Make Sure Tasks Get Done

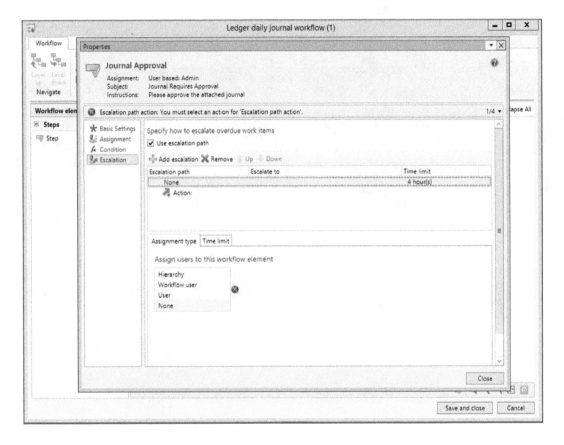

Click on the Add Escalation button within the Escalation tab to add your first person in the escalation process.

Use Workflow Escalation To Make Sure Tasks Get Done

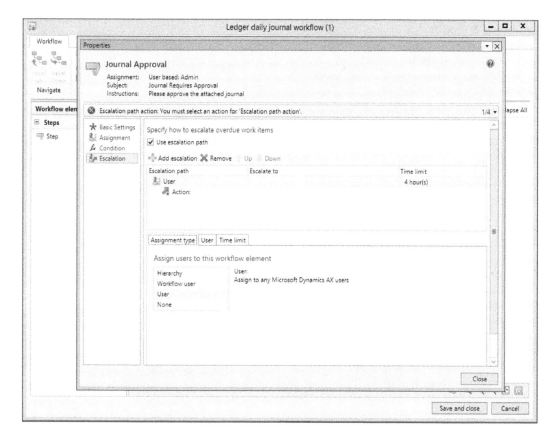

To escalate to another user, select the User option from the Assignment Type sub-tab.

Use Workflow Escalation To Make Sure Tasks Get Done

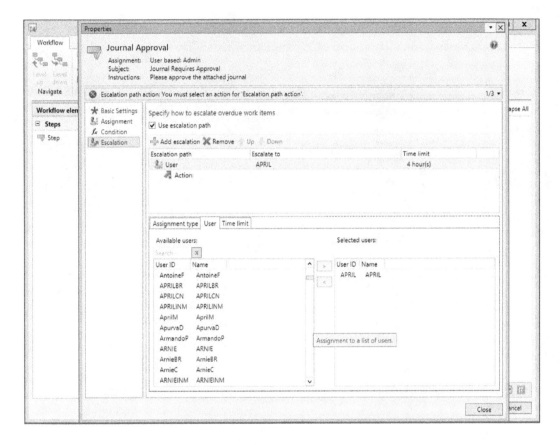

Switch to the User sub-tab, and select the user that you want to be notified when the original task has not been completed.

You can then switch to the Time Limit sub-tab as well if you want to adjust the time that is allotted for that user to act upon the escalated task.

Use Workflow Escalation To Make Sure Tasks Get Done

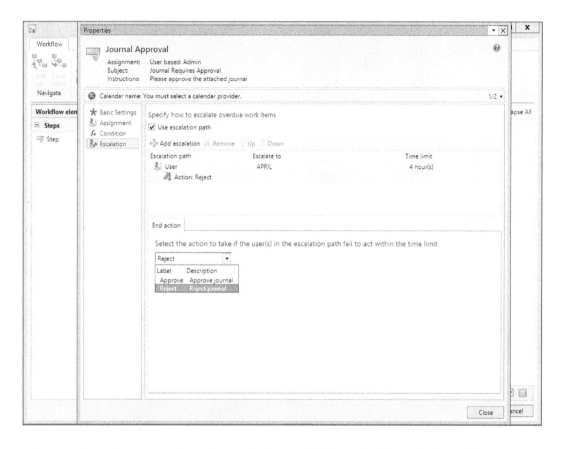

To complete the setup, select the Action item which is added by default to all escalation paths, and from the dropdown list, select the action that is to be performed when all escalations fail. In most cases the best choice is to err on the cautious side and select the Reject option.

After you have finished, you can click the Close button and activate the workflow.

Now when the workflow is processed, people will be motivated to act upon them ASAP.

Use Workflows Escalation Automatic Approval For Spot Reviews

You may think that the escalation rules can just be used to move a task up the corporate ladder when someone fails to pull their weight, but there is a kinder side of their nature as well. You can configure them to automatically approve tasks as well if they are not acted upon, making them a great way to have tasks assigned to users for review, but if they don't have the time to act upon them, or if they just want to periodically review transactions, then the tasks that they do not look at will continue on their merry way through the workflow.

It's just like throwing a D20 to see if your workflow is reviewed.

Use Workflows Escalation Automatic Approval For Spot Reviews

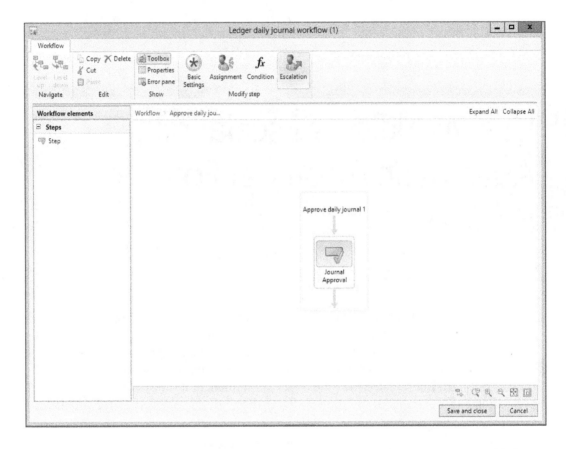

Open up your workflow design, and navigate to the element that you want to add the escalation rule to, and then then click on the Assignment button within the Modify Step group of the Workflow ribbon bar.

Use Workflows Escalation Automatic Approval For Spot Reviews

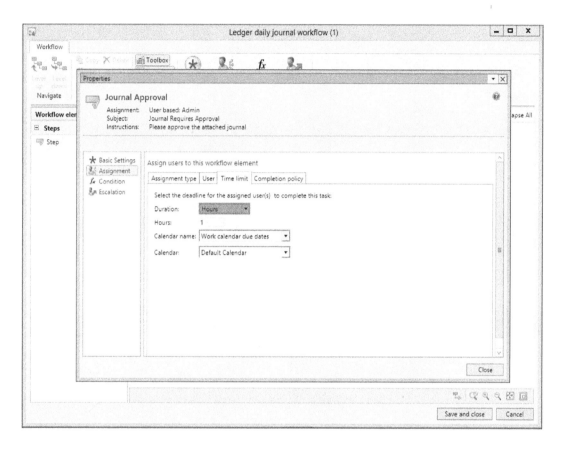

When the workflow step properties dialog box is displayed, select the Time Limit tab from the Assignment group, and set the time that you want task to be available for approval.

Use Workflows Escalation Automatic Approval For Spot Reviews

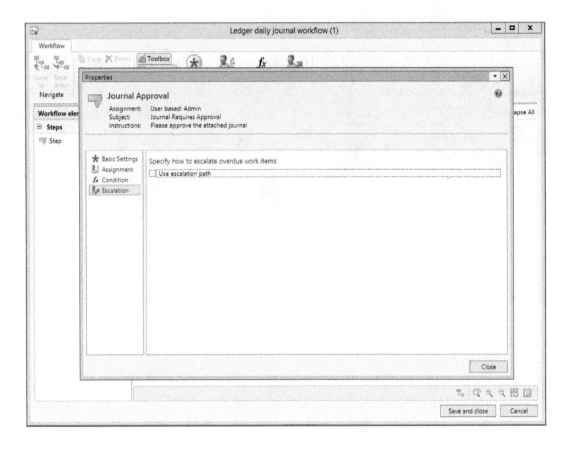

Now switch to the Escalation group, and check the Use Escalation Path checkbox to enable escalations.

Use Workflows Escalation Automatic Approval For Spot Reviews

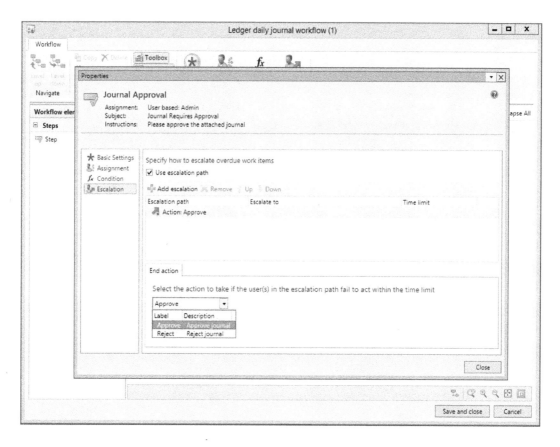

In this case, don't assign any more people to the escalation path, but select the Action line within the escalation rule, and set it to Approve.

Use Workflows Escalation Automatic Approval For Spot Reviews

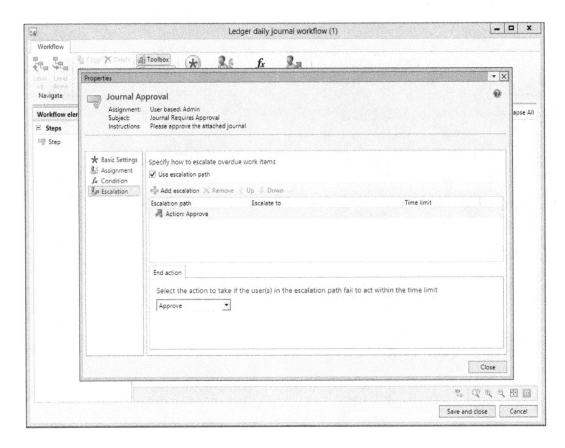

After you have finished, you can click the Close button and activate the workflow.

Now when the workflow is processed, the user that is assigned the task will have a set amount of time to review the transaction, and then if they do not act upon the task, then it will continue to the next step in the workflow.

SYSTEM ADMINISTRATION TIPS

There are a lot of ways that you can configure Dynamics AX as a System Administrator that make the application work even better. These configurations include archiving document, links to SharePoint, and also simplifying screens and portals for the users.

In this section we will show a few examples of how you can use these administrative tools to save time and make your life generally better.

Archive Excel Exports Automatically In SharePoint Document Libraries

When you export data from Excel, by default it creates a temporary export file locally on your workstation, although there is an option that you can use that will allow you to automatically archive the export to a default directory. This has the added benefit that you are also able to archive the files then to SharePoint. If you would like to make your exports sharable, or would just like to have a place to go to see all of the exports that you have done in the past, then this is a great option to configure.

You're not a data packrat if you do this...

Archive Excel Exports Automatically In SharePoint Document Libraries

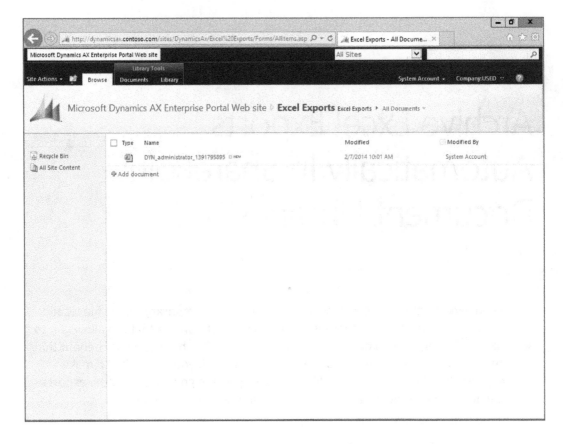

First, start off by creating a document library within SharePoint where you would like to archive off all of your exported files.

Archive Excel Exports Automatically In SharePoint Document Libraries

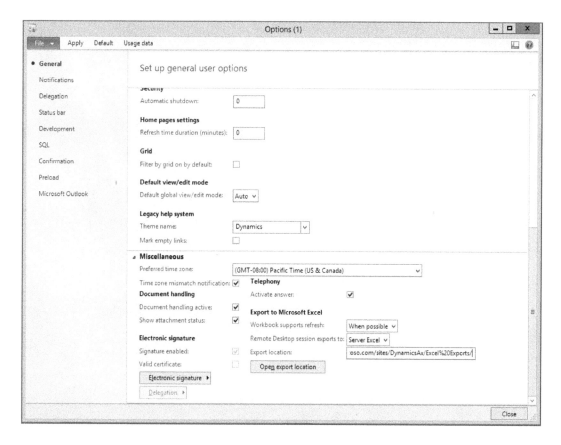

Then select the Tools menu item from the Options submenu of the Files menu.

Expand the Miscellaneous tab group and paste in the URL for your document library into the Export Location field. Make sure that you have the "/" on the end of the file path or else Dynamics AX will complain a little.

Archive Excel Exports Automatically In SharePoint Document Libraries

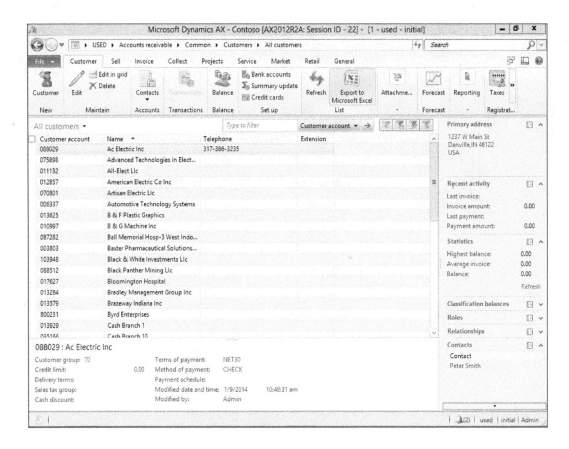

To see this in action, just export any data to Excel.

Archive Excel Exports Automatically In SharePoint Document Libraries

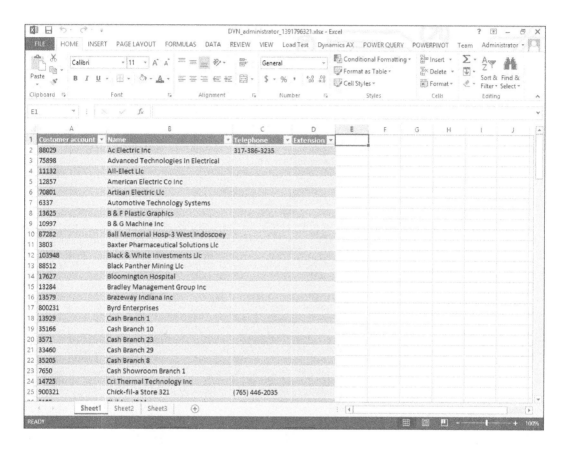

Your export will work exactly the same way as it did before...

Archive Excel Exports Automatically In SharePoint Document Libraries

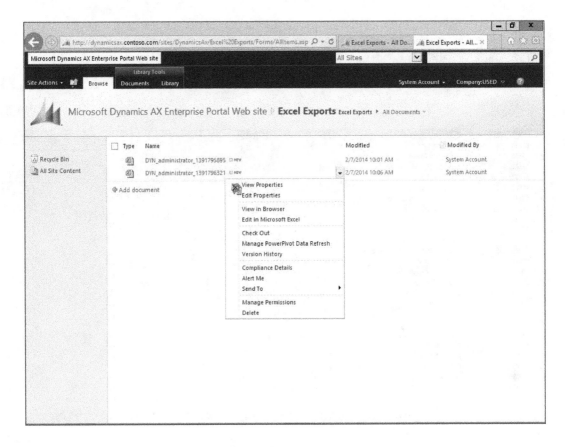

Although it will now use SharePoint as the archive for all of the documents.

Archive Excel Exports Automatically In SharePoint Document Libraries

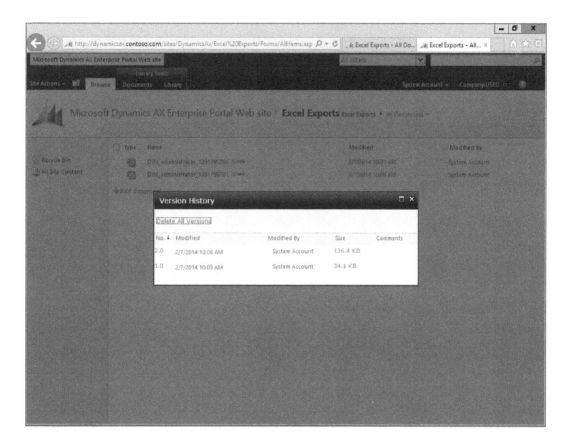

And also you will be able to see all of the version history of the document, including any changes that the user made when they manipulated the data... if you have version control turned on of course.

Share Your Screen Personalization With Other Users

If you have ever had a situation where another user has perfected the exact screen layout, and you want to use that same layout yourself, but don't have the time to personalize the forms, then don't worry. If you ask the user nicely they can save away that layout for you, and then you can apply it to your screens in a heartbeat through the personalization options.

Imitation is the sincerest form of flattery.

Share Your Screen Personalization With Other Users

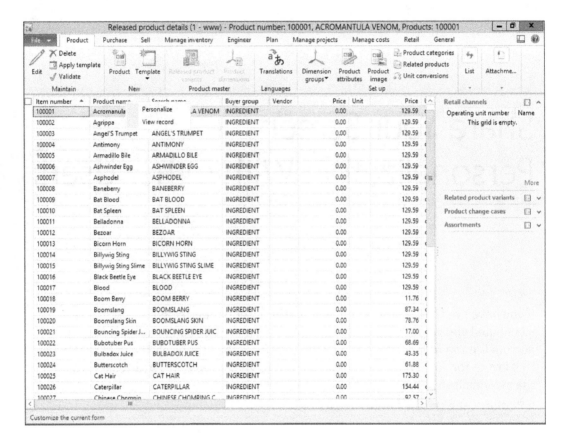

On the form that you want to share, right-mouse-click in the body, and select the Personalize option.

Share Your Screen Personalization With Other Users

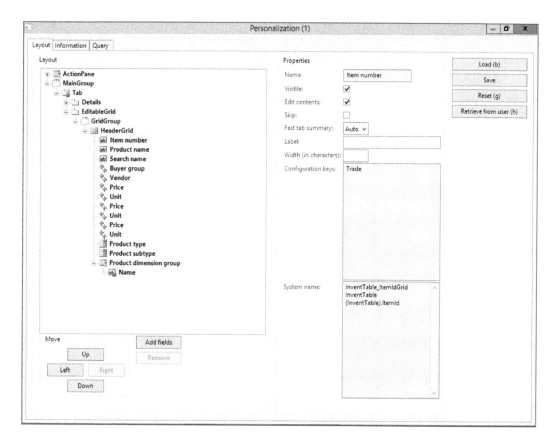

When the Personalization dialog box is displayed click on the Save button on the far right of the form.

Share Your Screen Personalization With Other Users

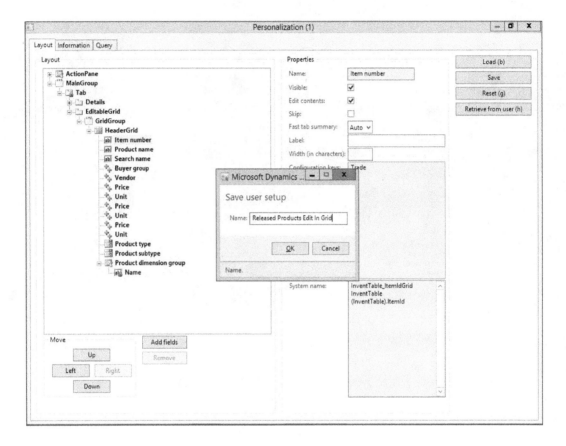

This will open up a Save user setup dialog box where you can give your saved screen layout a name and then click on the Close button.

Share Your Screen Personalization With Other Users

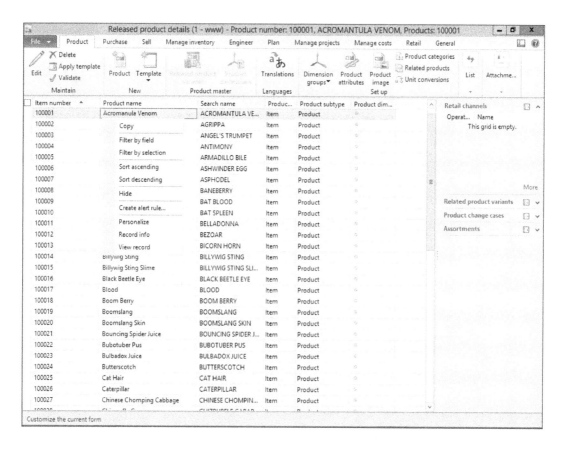

If a user likes you screen layout, and wants to quickly load the same configuration, all they need to do is open up the same form and then right-mouse-click on the body of the form so that the context menu is displayed. Then they need to select the Personalize menu item.

Share Your Screen Personalization With Other Users

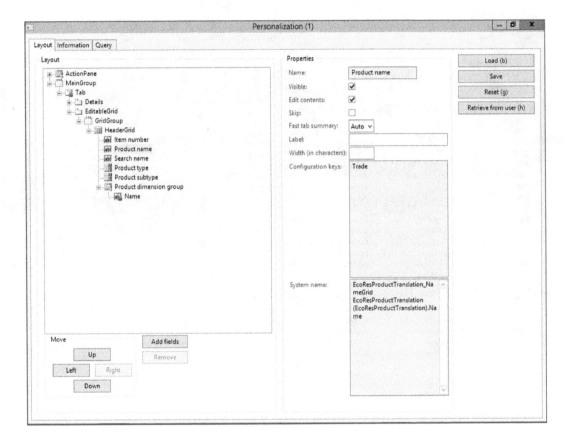

When the Personalization dialog box is displayed, they then should click the Retrieve from user button on the far right.

Share Your Screen Personalization With Other Users

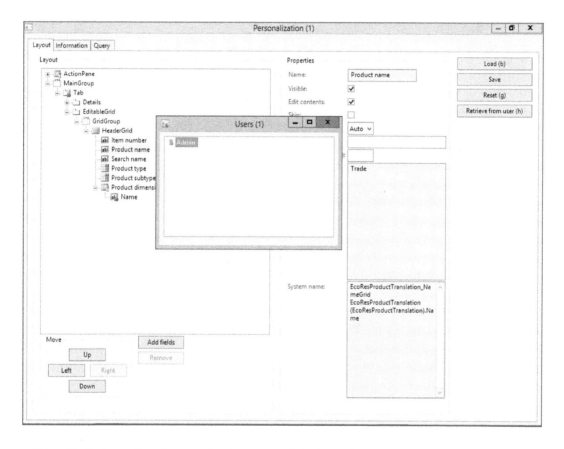

This will display a list of users that have saved their configurations that they can double click on.

Share Your Screen Personalization With Other Users

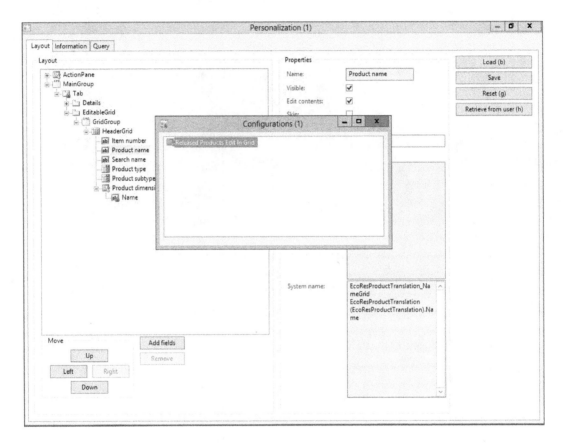

And then they will be asked which configuration they would like to copy (you can have multiple versions saved away).

Share Your Screen Personalization With Other Users

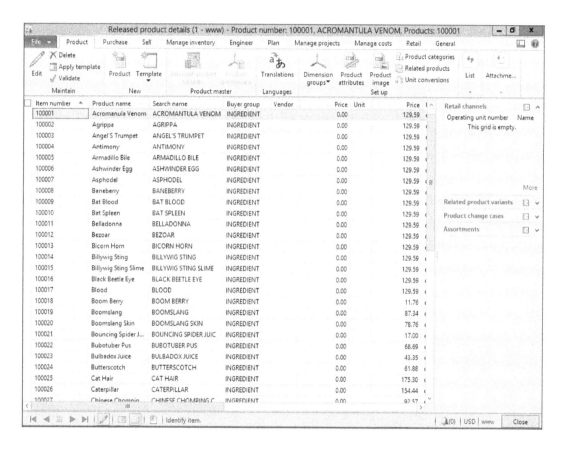

The next time that they open up the form, they will have the same format as the user that they copied the configuration from.

Archive Reports So That You Can Access Then Later On Without Rerunning It

When you rerun a report, there is a small chance that you will get slightly different report, because flags have been changed, or the report has been modified. If you want to preserve your report as it was when it was originally ran, then you can easily do that by saving it to the Report Archive. Once the report is archived, you can return to it over and over again without even rerunning it.

Now you have your very own microfiche system – minus the clunky reader.

Archive Reports So That You Can Access Then Later On Without Rerunning It

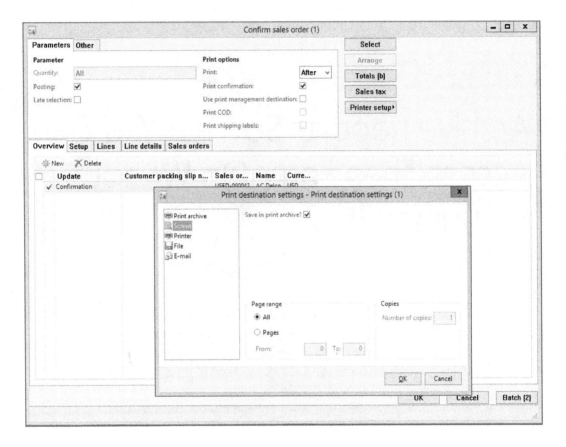

When you print any document, you may have noticed that there is a Save in Print Archive checkbox. To save the report to access later on, just check the box.

Also, if you always want to archive the documents, then you can set this as a default option within the Print Management.

Archive Reports So That You Can Access Then Later On Without Rerunning It

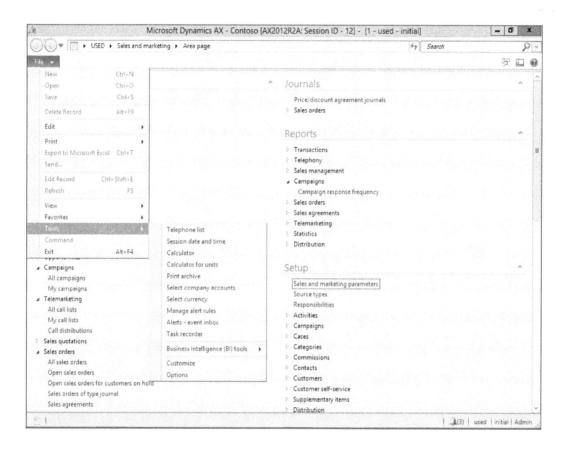

To view all of the archived documents, just click on the Files menu, select the Tools submenu, and then click on the Print Archive menu item.

Archive Reports So That You Can Access Then Later On Without Rerunning It

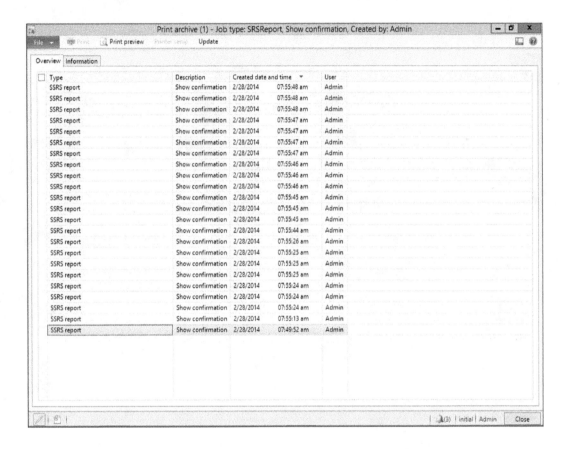

This will show you a list of all the reports that you have archived. To view the report, all you need to do is click on the Print Preview button within the menu bar.

Archive Reports So That You Can Access Then Later On Without Rerunning It

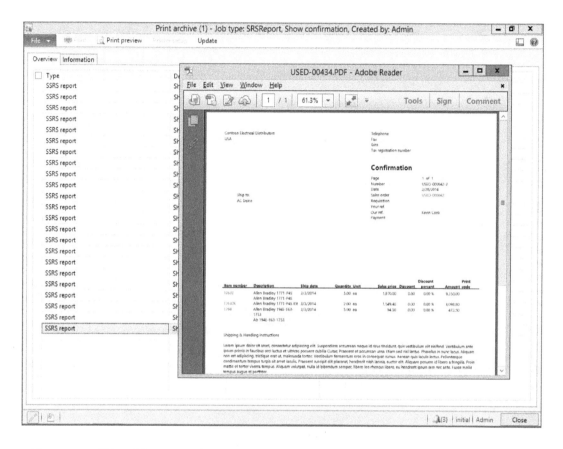

Then you will be able to see the original report.

Save Document Attachments To SharePoint

The document attachments function within Dynamics AX is super useful, but if you don't want all of the files that you attach cluttering up your database, or stored away on a local file share, there is another option available. You can save them off to SharePoint. This also has a side benefit of allowing you to take advantage of the features of SharePoint such as document control, versioning, and also workflow if you like to manage the processing of the attached documents.

Save Document Attachments To SharePoint

Before you start, make sure that you have a document library within SharePoint that you can save your documents to.

Save Document Attachments To SharePoint

The next step is to configure the Document Types so that they point to the SharePoint document library. To do that, click on the Document Types menu item within the Document Management folder of the Setup group within the Organization Administration area page.

Save Document Attachments To SharePoint

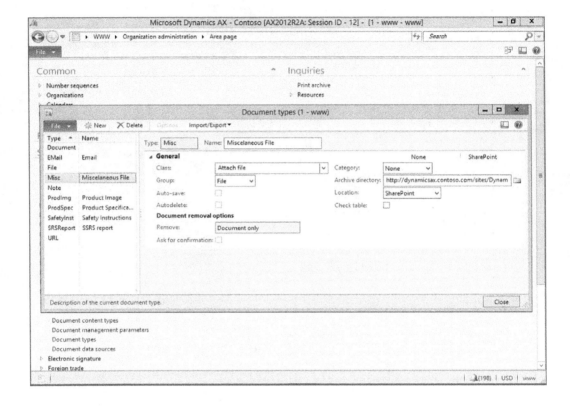

When the Document Types maintenance form is displayed, find the Document Type that you want to save to SharePoint, set the Location field to SharePoint and then paste in the URL for your SharePoint library into the Archive Directory field.

Save Document Attachments To SharePoint

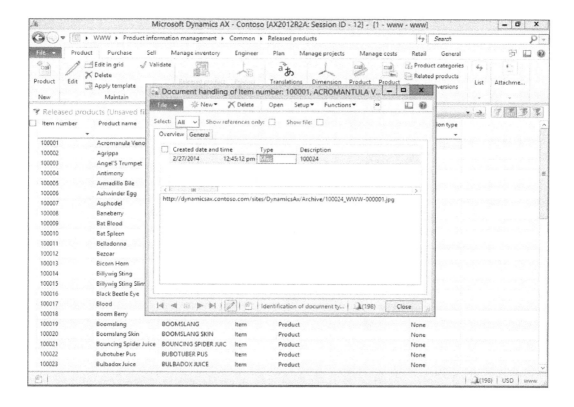

Now if you add a file as an attachment using that Document Type, it will save it to SharePoint, giving you a reference location for it in the notes.

Save Document Attachments To SharePoint

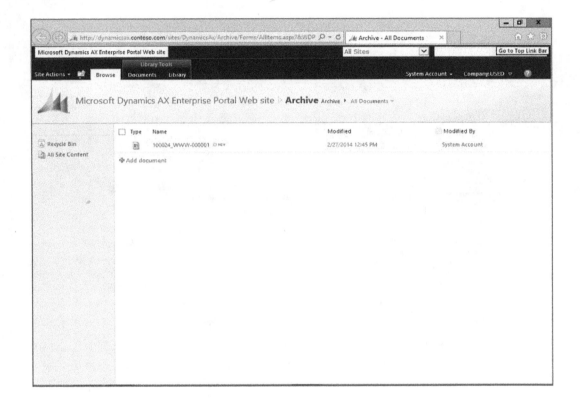

If you open up the SharePoint document library, you will see the file has been safely archived for you.

Creating Segregation Of Duties Rules To Block Possible Security Issues

There are two approaches to security that most people adhere to, the Lord Of The Fly's approach, or the 1984 approach. The first is where there is no security and the users will police themselves, and the second is where everything is controlled and monitored because the users cannot be trusted.

If you are in the latter camp when it comes to security, then you can even secure the security managers by implementing security rules that manage the security managers themselves through the Segregation of Duties functions within Dynamics AX.

Creating Segregation Of Duties Rules To Block Possible Security Issues

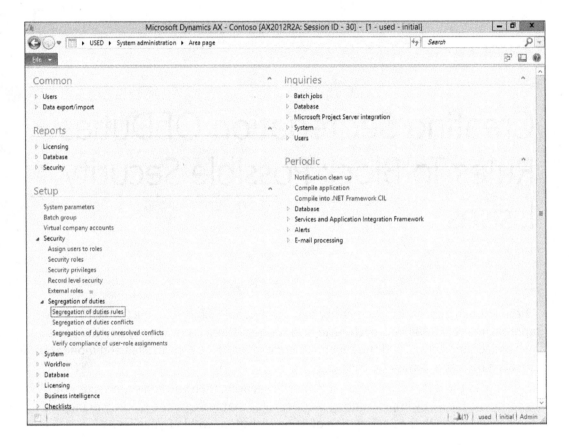

From the System Administration area page, click on the Segregation of duties rules menu item within the Segregation of Duties subfolder within the Security folder of the Setup group.

Creating Segregation Of Duties Rules To Block Possible Security Issues

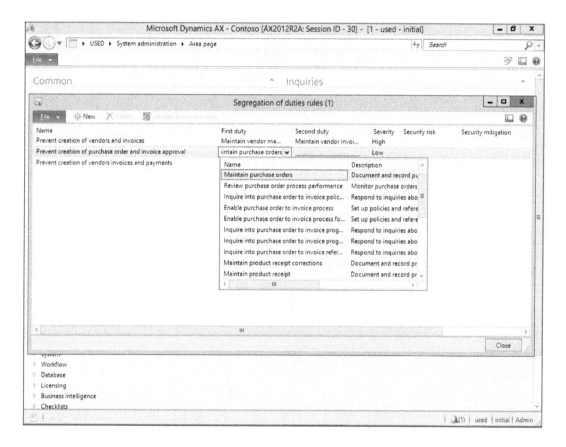

When the Segregation of Duties Rules maintenance form is displayed, click on the New button in the menu bat to create a new rule.

Then give your rule a Name and then select the First Duty for the rule.

Creating Segregation Of Duties Rules To Block Possible Security Issues

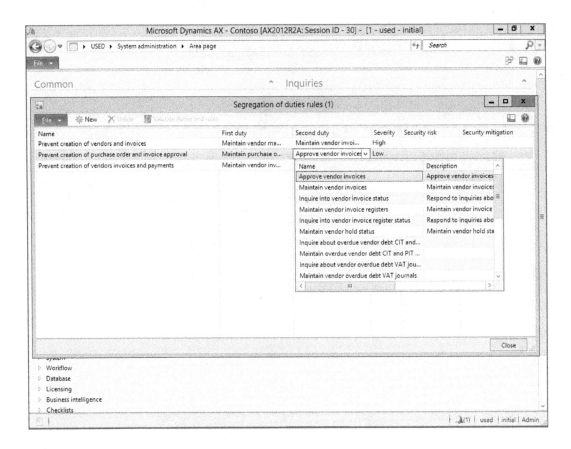

Then select the Second Duty that you do not want the users to have if they also have the first.

Creating Segregation Of Duties Rules To Block Possible Security Issues

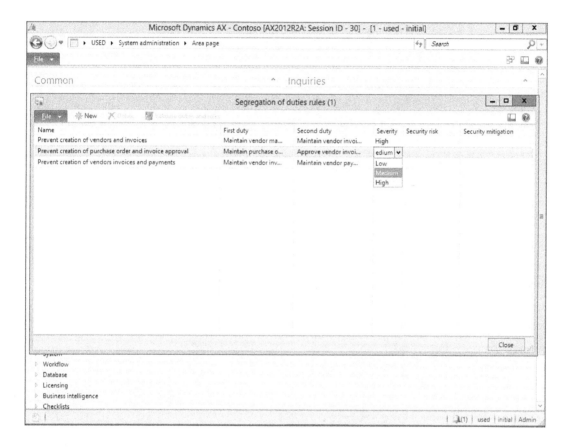

If you want, you can also assign a Severity level to the rule, because some infractions are not as serious as others.

When you are done, just click the Close button to exit from the form.

Creating Segregation Of Duties Rules To Block Possible Security Issues

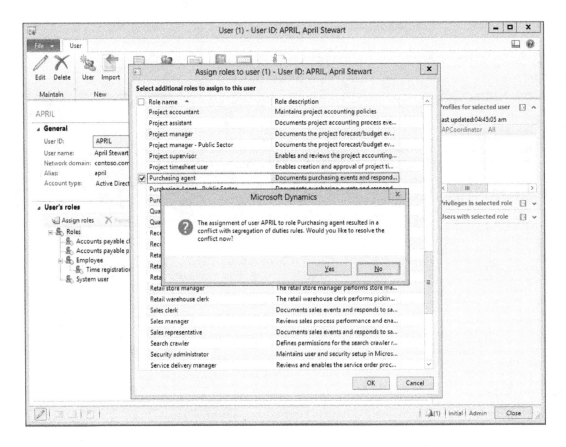

Now if anyone tries to tinker with the security and assign roles that give them questionable rights they will be notified of the conflict right away.

Now the watchers are being watched.

Hide The Parent Navigation Tabs To Tidy Up The Portal Navigation Bar

When you install the Enterprise Portals, by default, all of the sites are displayed within the navigation bar. This is OK if you only have a couple installed, but if you have them all up and running, and then start to create collaboration workspaces, the top navigation pane can quickly start chewing up your screen real-estate, and more importantly make the screen look untidy.

Luckily, since this is built on SharePoint, you can easily change the default settings so that you just see the current portal name in the navigation bar, an everything looks so much cleaner.

Hide The Parent Navigation Tabs To Tidy Up The Portal Navigation Bar

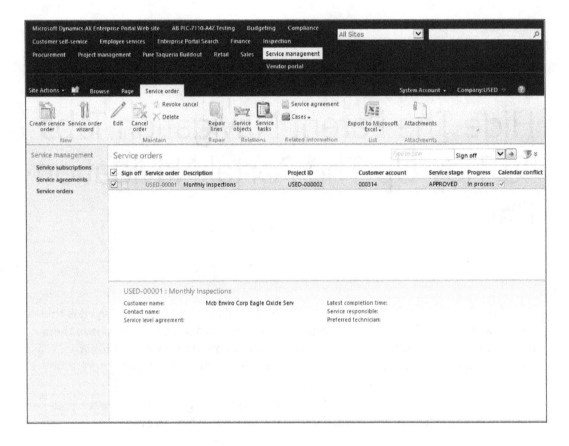

Philip K. Dicks Law of Kipple in action...

Hide The Parent Navigation Tabs To Tidy Up The Portal Navigation Bar

Click on the Site Actions menu item, and select the Site Settings menu item.

Hide The Parent Navigation Tabs To Tidy Up The Portal Navigation Bar

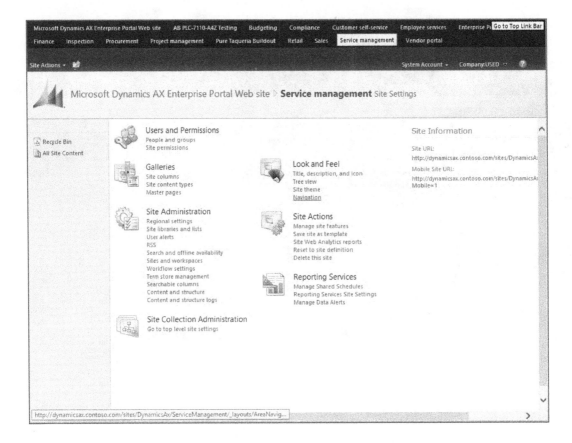

When the Site Settings menu is displayed, click on the Navigation menu item from within the Look and Feel menu group.

Hide The Parent Navigation Tabs To Tidy Up The Portal Navigation Bar

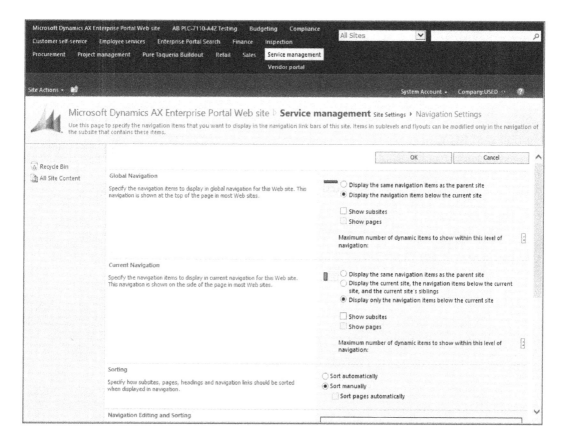

When the Navigation Settings options page is displayed, check the Display the navigation items below the current site radio button within the Global Navigation group and then click OK to save the preferences.

Hide The Parent Navigation Tabs To Tidy Up The Portal Navigation Bar

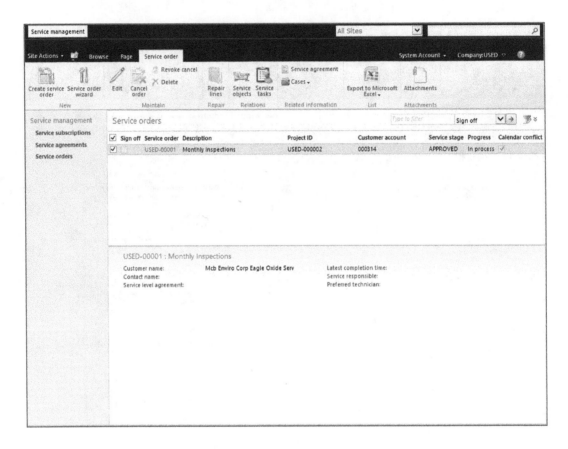

Now when you return to your portal, you will not see all of the other sites cluttering up your navigation bar.

SUMMARY

There are so many tricks and tips that you can take advantage of within Dynamics AX, that we cannot possibly inventory them all, but the ones that we have shown throughout this book are a good start.

About the Author

Murray Fife is a Microsoft Dynamics AX MVP, and Author with over 20 years of experience in the software industry.

Like most people in this industry he has paid his dues as a developer, an implementation consultant, a trainer, and now spend most of his days working with companies solving their problems with the Microsoft suite of products, specializing in the Dynamics® AX solutions.

EMAIL	murray@dynamicsaxcompanions.com
TWITTER	@murrayfife
SKYPE	murrayfife
AMAZON	www.amazon.com/author/murrayfife
WEB	www.dynamicsaxcompanions.com